The
LEMON
LOVERS
Cookbook

The LEMON LOVERS Cookbook

PEG BAILEY

Illustrations by Laura L. Seeley

LONGSTREET PRESS, INC.
Atlanta, Georgia

Published by
LONGSTREET PRESS, INC.
A subsidiary of Cox Newspapers,
A subsidiary of Cox Enterprises, Inc.
2140 Newmarket Parkway
Suite 118
Marietta, GA 30067

Printed in the United States of America
1st printing, 1996
Library of Congress Catalog Card Number: 96-76510
ISBN: 1-56352-324-8

This book was printed by Quebecor/Hawkins County.
Digital film prep and imaging by Advertising Technologies, Inc., Atlanta, GA
Jacket design by Jill Dible. Book design and typesetting by Laura McDonald.

To my son, Blair,
who considers food and cooking great fun,
and to all my fellow lemon lovers,
wherever they may be.

Contents

Acknowledgments

HOW DO YOU BEGIN TO THANK all the people who have given moral support, time and effort to help you put together a cookbook? Difficult, but I shall try through this medium to give credit and appreciation to all.

First, of course, there is Frank Hannegan, with his great cartoon talent and his biggest fan, Nancy. I would also like to thank Mary-Lin Jackson and Pete Maier, who wrestled with my initial scratchings; Jack Bailey, for going over the manuscript with his fine pencil; Jeff Marcus, a very talented young man; Mark and Carol Rollinson; Maisie Maguire; and Prudence Squier, all of whom gave so much help and encouragement.

My heartfelt thanks to my many supportive friends: Peggy Marcus, Jane Low, Peter Boyle, Mary Nelson, Kate Wallace, Maureen Grant, Sara Branson, Mini Walsh, Jack Bradley, Peter and Pat Healey, Howard and Lilliana Kay, Sara Nolan, Richard Greene, Cathy McCormick, Janet Boyle, Joe McCormick, Cynthia Fleming, and the members of my Washington Capital Speakers Class, who have given my life an extra dimension of good friendship and fun these past few years.

A very special thanks to Joyce LaFray, Phyllis Santa and Suzanne De Galan, who were responsible for getting this book to market. Suzanne, my editor, deserves a gold medal for her unfailing good humor and patience.

This book was written on my IBM Selectric typewriter. I love it; it thinks like I do. However, books these days are submitted on computer disks, and without the kind help of Bill McCormick, of Jordan Kitts Music, and his computer genius, P.J. Ottenritter, I would probably still be techno-illiterate and unpublished.

Most of all, I must thank my son, Blair, who in the main handled recipe-testing duties. His tolerance knew few bounds, and his help was unfailing. He's a young man with pretty good taste. He is a student at Villanova Law School but still finds time to cook for his new bride, Jessica, and my grandson, Charley, the border collie.

The LEMON LOVERS

Cookbook

Introduction

Modus Operandi, or How to Understand the Author and How She Operates in the Kitchen

I'VE ALWAYS LOVED LEMONS— they are so sunny, bright and versatile. Not many of nature's offerings can be used in everything from appetizers to desserts. There is little in the food world that a squeeze of lemon can't improve.

Perhaps this love affair grew out of a childhood in South Dakota, where fruit production was limited, produce was seasonal, canning was commonplace and a lovely bowl of lemons on the kitchen table in the middle of winter was a reminder that the sun and spring could not be far away.

Good food and eating were an integral part of my growing up, a product of good prairie stock, in a small town. I vividly remember the food I ate and the summer days of childhood spent peeling, chopping and cooking whatever was in season and needed preserving. Bushels of peaches for spiced peaches, peach jam and just plain peaches. Cucumbers for pickles. Tomatoes every which way, including green tomato relish.

My mother was French and Norwegian.

That meant a large garden, a strawberry patch, fruit trees and, of course, rhubarb plants. What we didn't grow we obtained from local farmers. South Dakota is not exactly a vegetable farmer's dream, so we made the most of what we had. Little was wasted, a habit my mother had learned while growing up as one of 12 children. She made her own catsup, pickles and head cheese!

In the spring we picked fresh asparagus. Strawberries came shortly after, if we were lucky enough to have avoided a late snowstorm or freeze. That meant strawberry shortcake and jams and jellies. And so it went from crop to crop as the summer progressed. From all this produce came pretty, wholesome meals. I don't remember eating canned tomato soup until much later in life, when living at a much faster pace. Always, my mother reached for a jar of home-canned tomatoes to make soup from scratch. Gradually, I developed my sense of taste and an appreciation of good food and the effort necessary to prepare it properly.

The kitchen was the center of our house when I was growing up, as it should be. In fact, in my opinion, houses should be built to surround kitchens. All I ever wanted to be was a good *baleboosteh* (queen of the kitchen in Yiddish). The world is never better than when I am busy in the kitchen, listening to wonderful music, preparing food to share with my family and friends. In fact, I taught my son to dance in the kitchen. The best heart-to-heart talks take place in the kitchen. Eating is a sensual experience, and while you don't have to be a true hedonist to appreciate it, it helps.

Anything to do with food always draws my attention. No matter where I am in the world, I always head first for the food places, such as markets and bakeries. This might mean the Berkeley Bowl in California or the food stalls next to the covered bazaar in Istanbul, Turkey. Food fascinates and excites me. A beautiful eggplant or a perfect apple can give me so much pleasure. Learning a new recipe or eating a new dish are simple adventures that give me great satisfaction.

I never stint on spending for good food, although I do search out sales. I almost never use imported, out-of-season produce in winter. I try to buy fresh, ripe and tasty fruits and vegetables in season and freeze for use in the colder months. When pressed for time, I often put whole, unpeeled peaches and tomatoes in heavy plastic food storage bags, seal well and freeze. Frozen peaches and tomatoes are so easy to peel before thawing that they don't even need blanching, and the flavor is better than canned. A fresh frozen peach is terrific with regular or frozen yogurt—almost as good as fresh.

Lately I have cut back on butter and cream. I have always loved olive oil and tend to use it instead of, or in combination with, butter in savory dishes. I subscribe to the Julia Child school of everything in moderation. I use butter and cream if it is necessary for the proper execution of a dish, but I attempt to eat less of them.

Sometimes I long for the good old days when I had plenty of time to putter in the kitchen. Now I must maximize my time and effort. If I am using mushrooms, I often clean and sauté extra to keep on hand for omelets, soups and sauces. When using ground beef, I make meatloaf, chili and meat sauce in one session. All freeze well. Making the most of your time in the kitchen will allow you to eat better food more often, particularly if you are a working parent. Who can afford to spend half of each day cooking anymore? Organization is the key, and of course the key to organizing is thinking and planning ahead. With practice you can invent all sorts of shortcuts and time-saving efforts suited to your lifestyle.

I love to entertain or just to have friends in for a family-style meal. People are so flattered to be asked to critique a trial recipe. Years ago, when my husband was involved with diplomats from many countries in Washington, D.C., and we entertained often, I developed certain menus and favorite dishes that I made over and over. I still make these same dishes, and my friends have come to expect the winter invites for lamb couscous, sauerbraten or a choucroute garnie. When summer comes, I bring out the salmon mousse and Salad Nicoise.

Some of the recipes in this book are based on old and favorite dishes of my childhood, others from dishes I have learned of in my travels around the world. Many recipes are strongly flavored but not especially exotic. I like a lot of lemon, so you must feel free to adjust the amount to suit yourself. I have made an effort to keep the recipes uncomplicated. I prefer to eat complicated dishes when dining out. It is such a treat to taste the new food combinations and ingredients found in many trendy restaurants. Some of these chefs are brilliant. Of course, once in your lifetime you should make a cassoulet or coulibrac just to prove you can do it.

My favorite cookbooks have always been the wives' club collections. No fancy pictures, but recipes that work and are pretty good! I can't tell you how many recipes in sophisticated new cookbooks can be found in one of my unpretentious compilations of twenty-five or thirty years ago. Many of my favorite recipes were adapted from recipes given to me over the years by friends. If you are generous and big hearted and have any recipes you'd like to share with fellow "foodies," send them along.

I have always maintained that a cookbook was worth buying if it added one or more wonderful, delicious and often-used recipes to a cook's repertoire. I can only hope that you find those gems in this book.

Lemon Basics

DOESN'T THE SIGHT OF LEMONS make you think of the beautiful blue skies of Greece, the light and sounds of the south of France, the overwhelming abundance of Italy, the warm sunshine of Spain and the turquoise coast and waters of Turkey? In fact, lemons make me think of sunny beaches and healthy living.

One must travel around the world to see the many uses of the lemon. In China and Morocco, lemons are preserved and used in various dishes. In India, lemons are pickled whole or soaked in spices and mustard oil. In Greece and Turkey, lemon garnishes most every plate. In Italy, people enjoy a lovely lemon liqueur called Lemoncello, which you can use in any recipe in this book that calls for spirits.

It takes only a small amount of lemon juice to provide a subtle dimension to an otherwise ordinary dish. Used judiciously, lemon will add an anonymous pungency. Lemon can be the predominant flavor in many wonderful condiments, desserts and main-course savory dishes, but, to my mind, its major claim to fame is as a flavor enhancer.

When cooking with lemons, the following hints will prove useful.

Lemon Tidbits

- When a recipe in this book calls for a lemon, it means a large lemon.
- One medium lemon = 3 tablespoons lemon juice
- One large lemon = 1/4 cup juice
- One medium lemon = 1 tablespoon grated lemon zest
- Buy lemons with smooth, firm skins. The thinner the skin, the more pulp and juice inside.

- Lemons will stay fresh at room temperature for about a week.
- Lemons will keep in the refrigerator for about six weeks if they are stored in a plastic bag.
- Always bring a lemon to room temperature before using its juice. Even better, put the lemon in boiling water or warm in the microwave for five to 10 seconds to make the juice flow.
- A good lemon juicer is essential. There are many, both manual and electric, on the market. Use a corrugated cone over a bowl or a French cone for small amounts. Use an electric juicer for large amounts. Black & Decker makes an inexpensive, well-designed small

juicer. Cutesy lemon squeezers are a waste of money.

- Always use freshly squeezed lemon juice. Never use the bottled or plastic containers. Frozen lemon juice is an acceptable substitute in some dishes. You may use frozen lemon juice in any recipes in this book that do not specify fresh.
- Lemon juice freezes very well. Measure 2 tablespoons into each compartment of an ice cube tray and freeze. When solidly frozen, empty the tray into a heavy plastic bag and store in the freezer. You will then have pre-measured lemon juice to use when cooking. You can also put one or two into a glass of cola or iced tea.
- The rind or yellow part of a lemon is called lemon zest. It has high concentrations of lemon oil and a much more intense flavor than lemon juice. It is best to remove zest before extracting the lemon juice. This can be done by using a special tool called a lemon zester or by using a swivel-handled vegetable peeler or by rubbing the lemon over a finely holed grater made of non-reactive metal. Be careful not to include any of the white underneath portion of the lemon, known as the albedo, or pith.
- For large amounts of zest, remove the

zest in strips with a vegetable peeler and pulverize in an electric spice grinder.

- Use fresh or frozen lemon zest, not dried. The dried lemon zest you find in the spice section of your supermarket will usually contain preservatives. If you have only dried lemon zest, reconstitute it with a bit of lemon juice before using. Sometimes recipes in this book require fresh, not frozen, zest. This is specified in the recipe.

- You may extract the lemon oil from the zest by coarsely chopping lemon zest, placing it on triple layers of cheesecloth and wringing the oil into a small container or directly onto sugar. This pure oil is very intense in flavor; a drop can go a long way, so use judiciously. I use an eye dropper to measure. You can now buy bottled, cold pressed lemon oil in specialty food stores at quite a fancy price. It is nice to have on hand for emergencies. Combine your lemon oil with other flavorings, such as garlic, basil or thyme.

- When cooking with any acid such as

lemon juice, always use nonreactive cookware, such as stainless steel, plastic or enamel-coated bowls, pots and pans. Using cast iron or aluminum will cause food to discolor and impart a metallic taste.

- Take care not to leave fish or meat in a lemon- or vinegar-based marinade too long. The lemon juice can partly cook or sear the flesh and cause it to break down.
- Use a mandoline slicer for thin lemon slices. If you don't have a mandoline, get one.
- Put squeezed lemon hulls in a plastic bag and freeze. Put them in your drinks or throw one or two into your soup pot. You can also grind them in the garbage disposal to keep it smelling fresh.
- Keep cut fruits and vegetables from browning by rubbing with lemon juice, or cover in a solution of 1 to 2 tablespoons lemon juice to a cup of water.
- Make lemon brandy to use in cakes and frostings by putting the zest of 2 lemons in $1/2$ cup of decent brandy. Let sit for at least a week at room temperature.
- Put lemon wedges into a bottle of vodka or gin and then place the bottle in the freezer. You'll have lightly lemon-flavored spirits (called "lead pipes" for short) in two weeks.

- Remove stains from white linens by rubbing the stain with a freshly cut lemon and placing the material in sunlight to dry. Beats bleach.
- If a recipe calls for buttermilk and you're fresh out, add a tablespoon of lemon juice to a cup of low-fat (1 percent) milk and let stand for 5 minutes. The resulting curdled liquid will work for cooking, but I don't recommend it for drinking.
- Rub your hands with lemon after cutting garlic or onions to remove the smell.
- Rub eggshells with a cut side of lemon before boiling to keep them from cracking.
- Put lemon peel in a 200°F oven for 15 minutes, and any unwanted odors will vanish.
- For the loveliest of centerpieces, cover a green foam cone (found at crafts stores) with lemons skewered on toothpicks. Put fresh parsley or white daisies between the lemons. Add the parsley or daisies at the last minute so they won't wilt.
- When making sweet whipped cream, add 1 to 2 teaspoons of lemon juice to 2 cups of whipped cream. You may

also add a half teaspoon of finely grated lemon zest for a more intense lemon flavor.

- Add a teaspoon or two of fresh lemon juice or a pinch or two of grated lemon zest to frozen dairy topping. You will be amazed at how the lemon perks up the flavor.
- Add a pinch of grated lemon zest to your pancake batter.
- Add grated lemon zest to your breakfast oatmeal or your oatmeal spice cookies.
- Add a bit of lemon zest to your meatloaf or meatball recipe.
- Rinse grapes in a lemon-water solution to remove any mold or fungus.

- To maintain maximum vitamin C content, use lemon juice immediately after squeezing.
- One tablespoon of lemon juice has only four calories, making it a wonderful tool for dieters.
- Lemon juice can make up for the absence of salt in a recipe.
- Lemons have no starch content.
- Lemons are high in potassium as well as vitamin C.
- The albedo, or white, underneath portion of the lemon (not used in cooking because it is bitter) is full of nutrients, particularly bioflavids. It contains fiber and pectin and is reputed to aid in digestion.

Lemon-Flavored Herbs

LEMON BALM is a member of the mint family. The leaves are lemon scented and are used in France to brew tisanes, which are aromatic teas meant to soothe the spirit. Lemon balm is also used in salads and in meat and chicken dishes.

LEMON VERBENA is the strongest of the lemon-scented herbs. It can be substituted for lemon grass in Asian recipes. It is used in sweet dishes and fruit salads. It is highly perfumed, so use carefully.

LEMON GRASS has a bulbous base that contains citral, one of the oils also present in lemon zest. It is this that gives lemon grass its sour lemon flavor. Lemon grass is used in Asian cooking, particularly Thai. Be sure to remove the herb from a dish before serving. The leaves can be infused in hot water to make teas. Lemon zest can substitute for lemon grass in a pinch.

LEMON THYME adds a hint of lemon to plain thyme. It is easy to grow. I prefer it to plain thyme in most dishes.

LEMON BASIL is a lemon-scented variety of basil. Love it. It will add an interesting dimension to your tomato sauce or other recipes calling for basil.

A Brief History of the Lemon

The cultivation of the lemon tree goes back some 2,000 years. It is native to Southeast Asia and believed to have originated in India. Lemons are grown extensively in the United States and Italy; other large producers are Spain, Greece, Turkey, Argentina and Chile.

The most common variety of lemon in the United States is the Eureka, followed by the Lisbon and Villafranca. These lemons have medium to thick skin, enabling them to withstand more handling and shipping. Other sweet lemon varieties from around the world include Marrakesh limonette, Mediterranean sweet and Millsweet. I have a Spanish pink lemon tree growing on my sun porch. These lemons are more acidic than, for instance, the Meyer lemon, a cross between a lemon and a mandarin, which originated in China. Unfortunately, the Meyer lemon is very thin skinned and does not ship well.

Meyer lemons, however, can easily be container-grown. Plant them in good, well-drained, sandy potting soil. Water when the top few inches of soil get dry and fertilize with a good container fertilizer. Dwarf Meyer lemon trees make neat little ornamental trees with thick, glossy leaves and pretty blossoms with a lovely scent.

You can also grow dwarf Ponderosa lemon trees in a tub. The fruit of this lemon tree is as big as a grapefruit, good and juicy, and the trees will bear fruit all year when placed in a warm, sunny spot.

Four Winds Growers (*P.O. Box 3538, Fremont, California 94539, 510/656-2591*) ships virus-free Meyer and Ponderosa trees and other dwarf-potted citrus trees. Send a stamped, self-addressed envelope for a booklet on how to grow your lovely lemon trees. Fruitful growing!

Lemon Pantry

PERHAPS BECAUSE lemons are so pretty and sunny, people love to give and receive gifts of food made with lemon. Many of the basic lemon recipes in the Lemon Pantry chapter make wonderful presents when put in decorative jars or bottles and tied with bows, or put in mason jars and covered with pretty flowered or gingham cloth covers. I have found that a nicely shaped bottle of vinegar filled with slices of lemon is particularly appreciated. Gifts of homemade lemon chutney, marmalade or lemon oil are all wonderful.

Lemon Syrup

Instead of buying cans of frozen lemonade, make a big batch of lemon syrup when lemons are cheapest (during the first part of the year) and keep in the refrigerator or freezer. You can also use lemon syrup to sweeten iced tea, add lemon flavor to a sweet dish or use as a syrup on pancakes and waffles.

ф∂

Combine water and sugar in a large saucepan. Cook over medium heat, stirring constantly, until sugar is dissolved. Add salt and lemon zest. Raise heat and bring to a boil. Boil for 5 minutes. Cool. Add lemon juice.

Refrigerate in a covered jar. Remove lemon zest before using. For lemonade, add 3 tablespoons lemon syrup to a glass of water or club soda. Garnish with fresh or frozen lemon slices. Add 2 to 3 tablespoons mashed fresh strawberries for a change of taste.

1 cup water

2 1/2 cups granulated sugar

Pinch of salt

Strips of zest from 4 lemons

3 cups fresh lemon juice

- Makes about 1 quart

Lemon Oil

Zest from 2 lemons

2 cups olive or vegetable oil

- Makes 2 cups

*Y*ou may have noticed the increasing number of expensive flavored oils appearing on your supermarket shelves. These oils are easy to make, and homemade oil is cheaper and certainly fresher. Use this delightful infused lemon oil in marinades, salad dressings and stir frys. You can add garlic or herbs for a more complex flavor. I make a lemon, garlic and red pepper oil that I use for stir-frying. I keep one jar of lemon olive oil for sautéing and one jar of lemon vegetable oil to use in baking; the latter adds a great, subtle flavor to cookies and cakes. Store this oil in the refrigerator and use within two to three months.

৪৯

Cut zest into small strips. Place zest and oil in a saucepan. Heat to temperature of 120°F. Cool to room temperature and pour into covered container to store. Store in a cool place.

When ready to use, strain desired amount using a small tea strainer.

Note: You can omit the heating of the oil and zest and simply add the lemon peel to the oil, but the flavor will not be as intense.

Lemon Vinegar

As with lemon oil, this vinegar is terrific in homemade salad dressing. In Eastern Mediterranean countries, people have been able to buy lemon vinegar in the stores for many years. Perhaps we shall too one day.

I like to make my lemon vinegar using seasoned rice wine vinegar. I try to keep four small jars of flavored vinegars on hand: plain lemon vinegar, lemon vinegar with garlic, lemon vinegar with tarragon and lemon vinegar with dill. For presents, I fill a tall decorative jar with fresh lemon slices, pour in lemon vinegar, cork and tie with a bow.

❧

Place lemon zest in a glass jar or bottle with a non-corrosive lid. (Or put plastic wrap between vinegar and metal lid.) Add vinegar. Allow at least five days for flavor to develop. You may refrigerate if you feel it necessary. I don't.

2 cups seasoned rice wine vinegar or white wine vinegar

Zest of 1 lemon

- Makes 2 cups

Lemon Pepper

Grated zest of 2 lemons

1 tablespoon coarsely ground
   black pepper

- Makes about 2 tablespoons

A jar of simple lemon pepper, made by you, and a bottle of commercially prepared lemon pepper should be mainstays in your spice cupboard. The prepared lemon and pepper seasoning found in the supermarket spice section usually contains other herbs and spices in addition to dried lemon zest and black pepper, so check the bottle. I am particularly fond of McCormick's no-preservative blend, which includes cumin, paprika, red pepper, oregano, thyme, garlic and onion.

ℰ

Dry zest for 20 minutes in a 200°F oven. Mix dried zest with pepper and store in an airtight container.

Note: You can dry the zest in the microwave for 2 to 3 minutes on high if you are in a hurry; however, I find the slower oven intensifies the flavor.

Lemon Butter

This is very handy to have in the refrigerator or freezer to use with meat, fish or vegetables, or even to make lemon garlic bread. When you need lemon butter, slice off a tablespoon or two and replace the roll in the freezer. Omit the parsley if you intend to keep for more than a week.

❧

Melt butter. Add lemon juice, parsley, zest, and white pepper. Pour into dish, cover, and store in refrigerator, or shape into a roll, wrap in wax paper, and freeze. Serve on cooked vegetables, fish, or pasta.

1 cup (2 sticks) unsalted butter

5 tablespoons fresh lemon juice

1/4 cup flat-leaf parsley, chopped

1 tablespoon grated lemon zest

Freshly ground white pepper to taste

- Makes 1 cup

Lemon Crumb Topping

Coarse bread crumbs

Grated Parmesan cheese

Minced garlic

Grated lemon zest

*L*emon crumb topping can turn an ordinary vegetable dish into something a bit more fancy for a dinner party. It adds an interesting taste and texture.

ℒↄ

Preheat broiler. Mix equal parts of all ingredients. Sprinkle over cooked eggplant, asparagus, cauliflower, fennel, or beans and broil for a minute or two until nicely browned.

Lemon Chutney

This lemon chutney is really very easy to make and goes wonderfully with fish, chicken, cold meats and vegetables. As you will note, there is no fat in this chutney, and a little spoonful can enliven a nonfat meal. Many people buy their chutneys and relishes even though they are simple to make. Making them yourself allows you to control the ingredients and have preservative-free foods. If nothing else, think of how virtuous you will feel and how pleased your friends will be to get jars of this as a gift. Chutney recipes are very flexible, and I hope you will feel free to change the seasonings to suit your tastes.

Remove the zest from the lemons. Cut away the white pith and discard. Finely chop the lemon zest and pulp. Mix lemon with salt. Let mixture stand overnight in a 2-quart stainless steel saucepan.

Next day, add remaining ingredients. Cook mixture gently, stirring, until thickened, 45 minutes to 1 hour. Pour into clean pint jars and refrigerate.

Let rest about a month before serving.

8 lemons

2 tablespoons salt

1 red onion, chopped

4 large cloves garlic, chopped

1 cup golden raisins

1 cup cider vinegar

1 tablespoon grated fresh ginger

1 teaspoon ground cloves

1/2 teaspoon ground cinnamon

1/2 teaspoon dried hot red pepper flakes

A 1-pound box brown sugar

- Makes 2 pints

Easy Lemon Mayonnaise

1 cup prepared mayonnaise

2 tablespoons olive oil

2 tablespoons lemon juice

1 teaspoon grated lemon zest

2 tablespoons chopped fresh chives (optional)

2 tablespoons chopped fresh parsley (optional)

- Makes 1¼ cups

My mother always made her own mayonnaise and also made a cooked dressing (see following recipe) for potato salad and coleslaw. Given time constraints, I simply doctor prepared mayonnaise to suit. Whisking in a bit of olive oil and lemon juice can turn even the most mundane, store-bought mayonnaise—especially low-fat, low-calorie versions—into an okay substitute for home-made. The little bit of olive oil and lemon juice add only a few calories and no saturated fat. For a more intense flavor, I add some lemon zest and, for variety, chives and parsley. It is best to make only as much as you need. Any leftover mayonnaise will keep about five days in the refrigerator.

೪๑

Beat olive oil into the mayonnaise until all the oil is incorporated. Beat in the lemon juice and add lemon zest. Stir in chives and parsley.

Cooked Lemon Mayonnaise

This recipe is based on my mother's. It will keep in the refrigerator for about five days. Remember, there are preservatives in the store-bought product that allow for room-temperature serving, but there are no preservatives in your homemade version, so serve cold.

ॐ

Combine egg yolks with cornstarch in a small saucepan. Add olive oil in a slow, steady stream, whisking constantly until all the oil is incorporated and the mixture is fully emulsified. Whisk in sugar, hot water, lemon juice, and lemon zest. Cook mixture over low to medium heat, whisking constantly, until thickened and mixture registers 160°F on a candy thermometer. (If you make this often, you will soon know when it is thick enough.) Season to taste with salt and pepper. Cool to room temperature. Refrigerate. Serve cold.

4 large egg yolks

1 tablespoon cornstarch

1/4 cup olive oil

1 tablespoon granulated sugar

1/2 cup hot water

3 tablespoons fresh lemon juice

1 tablespoon grated lemon zest

Salt and freshly ground white pepper to taste

- Makes 1 cup

Preserved Lemons

8 lemons, washed and dried

1/2 cup coarse salt, more if desired

Fresh lemon juice as needed

- Makes 8 Preserved Lemons

Several years ago, I was fortunate enough to wander through the souks of Morocco with a very knowledgeable guide, sampling the spices and the food. I learned that preserved lemons are one of the most important ingredients in many Moroccan dishes. The chopped rind provides a unique taste and texture to chicken and lamb stews and even to salads. You can add it to noodles and rice, or to anything your cook's heart desires.

Several countries, including India and China, have their own versions of preserved lemons; the Indian version includes cardamom pods. Other versions include cinnamon sticks, cloves, coriander seeds, black peppercorns and bay leaf.

The lemons will keep for up to a year in a cool place. The white substance you sometimes see in the jar is harmless. Since this version should sit for about 30 days before using, I have also provided a quick version. These lemons make a nice gift, packed in a quart jar with bay leaves to add color.

&

Without cutting all the way through, cut each lemon lengthwise into quarters, leaving them attached at one end. Sprinkle salt on each quarter. Place 1 tablespoon of salt in the bottom of a sterile quart mason jar and pack in the lemons, pushing them down to release the juice. If the released juice does not completely cover the lemons, add additional lemon juice. Leave some air space.

Cover and store at room temperature, shaking the jar every day for about 30 days.

Before using, rinse the lemons well. Cut away and discard the pulp. Chop the rind before adding to recipes.

Fast Preserved Lemons (2 to 3 Days)

Place lemons in a saucepan with salted water to cover. Bring to a boil. Reduce heat. Cover and simmer for 10 minutes.

Remove lemons from the pan. Cool.

Without cutting all the way through, cut each lemon lengthwise into quarters, leaving them attached at one end. Sprinkle inside of quarters with a teaspoon or so of salt and close sections back together. Pack lemons in a sterile pint jar, pushing to release juice. Cover. Allow to sit for 2 to 3 days before using. Use as above.

FAST PRESERVED
  LEMONS

4 lemons, washed and dried

1/4 cup coarse salt

Lemon Marmalade

3 large lemons

Water

1 cup granulated sugar, or more
    to taste

- Makes about 1 cup

I find most commercially prepared marmalades to be too sweet, including those made in the land of all marmalades, England. This recipe is easy to make and worth the trouble. It's tart, but feel free to increase the sugar amount. Many people don't like marmalade because it is bitter; however, if you take a bit more time and cut away the white of the lemon before making it, it can be less bitter. Try this on cinnamon raisin muffins or bagels.

❧

Zest the lemons. Cut away the white pith and discard. Coarsely chop the lemon pulp. Measure the combined pulp and zest.

Place in a glass or stainless steel bowl. Add an equal amount of water. Let stand overnight in a cool place, covered. Next day, boil mixture for 10 minutes, uncovered. Let stand overnight again.

Next day, heat. Add sugar. Boil, stirring until sugar dissolves. Let mixture reach the jelly stage on a candy thermometer (220°F), about 45 minutes. Pour into a sterile half-pint jar and cool. Cover and store in a cool, dry place.

Lemon Sugar

Use lemon sugar in your baking, for hot or iced tea, sprinkled on fresh fruit and in place of your regular sugar with morning cereal. You can now find lemon-flavored powdered sugar on the shelf at your grocery store. It is much better to make your own. It's fresher and the flavor is certainly better.

Lemon Granulated Sugar

Air dry lemon zest for a few hours on a sheet of wax paper. This dries the zest and prevents the sugar from lumping. Mix sugar and zest.

Lemon Powdered Sugar

Follow the directions for granulated sugar. You may find that the powdered sugar lumps from moisture in the lemon zest. Just whirl in the blender or break up with a fork.

Note: These sugars will keep for months in glass or plastic airtight containers. Be sure to remove zest from the sugar before using and return it to container. Use your judgment as to when to add more lemon zest, depending on your sugar use. The longer the lemon zest is in the sugar, the more intense the flavor will be. I keep flour shakers full of both powdered and granulated sugars to sprinkle on cakes, cookies and the like.

GRANULATED SUGAR

2 cups granulated sugar

Zest from 2 lemons

- Makes 2 cups

POWDERED SUGAR

A 1-pound box confectioners' sugar

Zest from 2 lemons

- Makes 2 cups

Appetizers

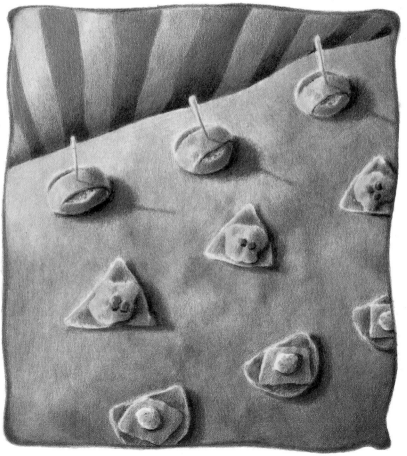

I OFTEN THINK of a meal as a symphony that moves from prelude to finale. Appetizers are the prelude and are meant to stimulate the appetite. Nowadays, the term *appetizer* is almost synonymous with hors d'oeuvres. I rather like the British term *starter*, used when the appetizer is the first course of a meal as opposed to small bits of food taken with before-meal aperitifs or drinks. Personally, I can quite happily make a meal of appetizers. It's good fun to sample a small bit of many different dishes (particularly when someone else has prepared them).

You may remember the days of stand-up cocktail parties, with all their potato chips, dips, meatballs, stuffed mushrooms, cheese logs and so on. Many of these tidbits, along with hard liquor, are out of favor. The cocktail buffet table now includes raw vegetables, yogurt dips and fat-free crackers. I do find that people nowadays simply don't want as much to eat, so if I do a starter, I often prepare no more than a light soup or salad. If it is a weekend and people are relaxed and a little off their diets, I will serve some light munchies with a glass of wine or champagne before lunch or dinner.

These appetizer recipes are not difficult to make, have no pretense to haute cuisine and have served me in good stead for many years. Probably my all-time-favorite, no-recipe-needed appetizer is pieces of prosciutto wrapped around bite-sized pieces of melon. Spear them on toothpicks, place on a pretty plate, squeeze lemon juice over all and serve. People love it! Another of my easy, best-loved, fast appetizers is cherry tomatoes and black olives (preferably oil-cured), tossed together with fresh lemon juice and a bit of olive oil. Serve on a lettuce-lined plate with toothpicks. Learn to make simple dishes to please your family and friends, then experiment, trust your taste buds and make these recipes your own.

Vegetable Tempura

1 cup all-purpose flour, sifted twice

Pinch of baking soda

Pinch of salt

1/4 teaspoon garlic powder (optional)

1 egg

1/2 cup fresh lemon juice, well chilled

Water to thin batter, if necessary

Vegetable oil, preferably peanut oil, for frying

Vegetables such as asparagus, onions, and zucchini, cut into pieces and well dried

- Serves 4

As I recall, I first had tempura at the Pearl City Tavern shortly after marrying and moving to Hawaii. The PCT had a great long bar backed by a huge cage of wonderful monkeys. Nothing like sipping on your Mai Tai and talking to the monkeys, then adjourning to a table to have some Japanese food and a few Island specialties such as grilled mahi-mahi. I also learned to love sashimi at the PCT. All of this was back before Hawaii became overbuilt and overrun with tourists; life was laid back, the way it should be in paradise.

You can make the tempura batter from scratch using the recipe below or, if you are in a hurry, use a tempura

mix and substitute lemon juice for some of the water. I like to make vegetable tempura, but you can certainly use this batter for shrimp, scallops or pieces of fish fillet. Again, you can make your own dipping sauce or purchase one in a bottle. The one absolute is that you serve the tempura immediately; it does not bear waiting or warming.

Mix flour, baking soda, and seasonings. Beat egg until light colored. Stir in lemon juice. Combine flour mixture with egg mixture. Batter may be a bit lumpy. Let sit while heating oil.

Heat at least 4 inches of oil to 375°F in a deep fryer or deep, straight-sided skillet.

Dip vegetables in batter and fry in hot oil until golden brown. Drain on paper towels. Serve immediately with dipping sauce.

Dipping Sauce

Combine all ingredients.

Note: You can strain cooked oil and store in covered jar in refrigerator for reuse.

DIPPING SAUCE

1/2 cup soy sauce

1/2 teaspoon finely grated fresh ginger

1 tablespoon finely minced green onion

1 tablespoon sake (optional)

1 teaspoon prepared horseradish (optional)

Mushrooms à la Grecque

2 pounds whole mushrooms, 1 to 1½ inches in diameter

2 cups water

1 cup olive oil

¼ cup fresh lemon juice

3 cloves garlic, quartered

1 branch fresh fennel, cut up, or 2 tablespoons dried fennel seed

¾ teaspoon ground coriander

10 peppercorns

5 sprigs lemon thyme or thyme or ½ teaspoon dried thyme

½ teaspoon dried sage

1 bay leaf

½ teaspoon dried rosemary

1 stalk celery, cut up

1 teaspoon salt

• Serves 8 to 10

A la Grecque means fixed in the Greek way. If you have a problem with saying it, you may just say marinated mushrooms. This is a great, light and easy appetizer or meal accompaniment. I always try to have some in the refrigerator during the summer months, but they are good any time. I find people on a diet scoop them up. They are certainly healthy, and elegant to serve as well. You can substitute other vegetables such as artichoke hearts, celery or fennel; adjust the cooking time accordingly. Serve at room temperature on a bed of greens with toothpicks.

❧

Clean mushrooms and set aside.

Combine all the ingredients except mushrooms in a large, stainless steel saucepan. Bring to a boil. Simmer 10 minutes. Add mushrooms. Cook, stirring occasionally, for about 10 minutes, or until mushrooms are barely tender. *Do not overcook.*

Pour into a bowl and marinate overnight in refrigerator. Mushrooms can stay in marinade a week or so. They'll get better every day. To serve, remove mushrooms from marinade. Serve at room temperature. Check for seasoning before serving. You may wish to sprinkle with salt.

Ribs to Remember

These ribs will knock your socks off. They're completely different from anything you have ever tasted. You may cut them into serving pieces before marinating. This makes it easier to put them into a resealable plastic bag to marinate. Tamari is a richer, mellower version of soy sauce, naturally brewed and aged. You can now find it in most supermarkets.

ફ્રcapital

Mix all of the ingredients except spareribs. Cut spareribs into sections or serving pieces if desired. Place in a glass baking dish or plastic bag. Pour marinade over all. Refrigerate for at least a day, 2 days will be even better.

Preheat oven to 300°F. Remove ribs from marinade. Put in baking pan. Bake for about 3 hours until nicely browned, siphoning off accumulated fat from time to time.

Serve at room temperature with lots of napkins.

2 cups olive oil

1 cup tamari sauce

8 tablespoons honey

2/3 cup fresh lemon juice

1 tablespoon freshly ground black pepper

12 large cloves garlic, chopped

2 sides of spareribs, about 10 pounds in all

- Serves 6 to 8

Rillettes de Saumon

A ½-pound salmon fillet or steak, skinned and cut into 4 pieces

¼ teaspoon salt

2 tablespoons (¼ stick) unsalted butter

1 large shallot, minced

2 tablespoons dry white wine or dry vermouth

6 tablespoons (¾ stick) unsalted butter

¼ pound smoked salmon, diced

2 tablespoons extra-virgin olive oil

1 egg yolk

2 to 3 tablespoons fresh lemon juice

⅛ teaspoon freshly ground black pepper

Freshly grated nutmeg to taste

• Serves 6

A rillettes mixture resembles a pâté and can be made from meat—usually pork, but sometimes poultry or fish. This recipe is a combination of fresh and smoked salmon, which is pulverized and packed in a small container or pot, sealed with a thin layer of butter and kept in the refrigerator. I was assigned to make this recipe for our gourmet club's summer picnic years ago and have been making it ever since. You may omit the raw egg yolk, and the recipe won't suffer too much. Serve the rillettes with La Rotie (French for "roasted"). If you do not use all the rillettes, cover with a thin film of fat and store for two or three days in the refrigerator.

❧

Sprinkle salt on fresh salmon. Let stand at room temperature for 20 minutes.

Heat 2 tablespoons butter in skillet large enough to hold salmon. Add shallots and cook over medium heat, about 3 minutes. Add wine, then salmon. Cook, turning once, until opaque, about 4 minutes depending on the thickness of the salmon. Remove and cool, reserving pan liquid.

Flake salmon. Mix with reserved pan liquid. Dice 6 tablespoons butter. Place in food processor fitted with plastic blade. Add cooked salmon and smoked salmon. Pulse until ingredients are combined. Keeping machine running, quickly add olive oil, egg yolk, and lemon juice. Stop machine. Do not puree.

Add black pepper and nutmeg. Taste. Add salt if necessary. Pack into a small crock. Use within 2 or 3 days.

La Rotie

Preheat oven to 400°F. Slice bread into thin slices. Brush both sides of bread with olive oil. Sprinkle one side with herbes de Provence, that wonderful mixture of bay leaf, thyme, rosemary, basil, coriander, nutmeg, savory, lavender, and cloves. Or sprinkle with any herb of your choice, or top with grated lemon zest.

Place in a single layer on baking sheet. Bake about 5 minutes, or until crisp and golden.

LA ROTIE

Loaf of French bread

Olive oil

Herbes de Provence or herbs of your choice

Grated lemon zest (optional)

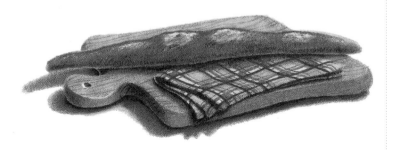

Marvelous Mussels

8 pounds mussels

4 tablespoons (1/2 stick) unsalted butter

2 cups dry white wine

1/4 cup fresh lemon juice

1/2 cup minced shallots or green onions

4 sprigs fresh parsley

1 bay leaf

4 cloves garlic, chopped

1/2 teaspoon dried thyme

Freshly ground black pepper

- Serves 8

*T*here are no mussels in South Dakota, so it was not until life with the U.S. Navy took my husband to Europe that I encountered this delectable food. We were visiting some friends in Brussels (the mussel capital of the world, they claim), and we all took ourselves down to the Grand Place to Chez Leon and ate huge platters of fresh, wine-steamed mussels. It was instant love. Happily, you can now find farm-raised, pre-scrubbed mussels in your supermarket, so you need only debeard with a sharp knife. It is a good idea to soak the cleaned mussels in a bowl or sink of water for two hours or so to rid the shells of sand. Discard any mussels that are not tightly closed. Rinse again and drain and you are ready to cook.

※

Scrub and debeard mussels. Put all the ingredients except the mussels in a 10-quart kettle with cover. Boil for 3 to 4 minutes. Add mussels. Cover and cook for about 5 minutes over high heat, shaking the pan frequently. Discard any mussels with unopened shells. Scoop out the mussels into soup bowls and ladle liquid over the top. Serve immediately with lots of good bread to soak up the juice.

Crabmeat Spread

I had a hard time deciding whether to include this recipe or crab cakes, but in the end this simple spread for crackers won. Lemon juice lightens the richness of the crabmeat. This spread can also be topped with Lemon Crumb Topping (see recipe page 26) and popped in the oven for half an hour to make a nice, hot appetizer or entree. A bit easier than frying crab cakes.

❧

Whisk lemon juice into mayonnaise. Combine mayonnaise and the remaining ingredients except paprika and parsley. Mix well. Put in a pretty bowl. Cover. Chill well.

Sprinkle with paprika and chopped parsley before serving.

1 cup mayonnaise, regular or low-fat

1/3 cup fresh lemon juice

1 pound fresh lump crabmeat, well picked over

5 or 6 green onions, minced

1 cup minced red bell pepper

1 can water chestnuts, drained and minced

Salt and freshly ground black pepper to taste

Paprika and chopped fresh parsley to garnish

- Serves 4 to 6

Guacamole

STANDARD

1 small onion, cut into pieces

3 ripe avocados, peeled and cut into large chunks

2 teaspoons fresh lemon juice

1 1/2 teaspoons chili powder

1 1/2 teaspoons ground cumin

Salt to taste

1 medium tomato, chopped

- Serves 6

BILL MAGUIRE'S

1 large ripe avocado, peeled

2 small center stalks of celery with leaves, finely minced

2 or 3 cherry tomatoes, finely chopped

1 tablespoon mayonnaise

1 teaspoon fresh lemon juice

1 tablespoon balsamic vinegar

Shake of garlic salt

Salt and freshly ground black pepper to taste

- Serves 2 to 3

*G*uacamole is perhaps the most famous dish made with the mild and nutty-flavored avocado. Is there anyone who doesn't like "guac"? I first had this dish at the race track in Tijuana, so many years ago I'm afraid to tell you. Since then it has been a staple at every Sunday football viewing in my house. I am giving you two versions. Just remember to use ripe avocados. Since they are usually hard when you buy them, plan ahead a bit and put your avocados in a brown paper bag for a couple of days to ripen.

Standard Guacamole

Pulse onion in food processor until finely chopped. Add avocado chunks, lemon juice, and seasonings and pulse.

Add chopped tomato. Pulse once or twice. Taste for seasoning. Add more chili powder or salt if needed. Serve with tortilla chips.

Bill Maguire's Guacamole

Mash avocado. Add remaining ingredients. Taste for seasoning. Serve with tortilla chips.

Hummus

Not too long ago, while having dinner at L'Auberge Provençale in Clarke County, Virginia, I found hummus on the menu. How far we have come when this Middle Eastern dish made from common chick peas, lemon juice, garlic and oil makes it onto the menu of this elegant French country inn. Granted, it wasn't your everyday garden-variety hummus, so of course I simply had to adjust my recipe to include what I thought Alain put in his. Comes close. I have used olive oil instead of sesame oil only because more people commonly have that in their pantry, and if I wait for you to go out and buy some, you'll never make the dish. Serve with warm pita bread.

୧ର

Put all ingredients except parsley, green onion, and tomato in food processor. Blend until smooth. You may add more lemon juice or olive oil to achieve desired dipping consistency. Taste for seasoning.

Stir in chopped tomato and green onion. Top with chopped parsley.

A 20-ounce can chick peas, drained

1/2 cup extra-virgin olive oil

1/2 cup fresh lemon juice

3 cloves garlic, chopped

2 teaspoons cumin

1 teaspoon salt

3 green onions, minced

1 small tomato, seeded and chopped

1/4 cup finely chopped fresh parsley

- Makes 1 3/4 cups

Hot Artichoke Dip

A 14-ounce can artichoke hearts, drained thoroughly and coarsely chopped

1 cup mayonnaise, regular or low-fat

1 cup grated Parmesan cheese

2 to 3 tablespoons fresh lemon juice

A 4-ounce can chopped green chilies, drained

Garlic salt to taste

Lemon Pepper (see recipe page 24) to taste

- Serves 8 to 10

I have wonderful Greek friends who own an artichoke farm outside the village of Iria, Greece. My friend Adriani makes many wonderful dishes using fresh artichokes and lemon. When I go to that part of the world I will have artichokes fixed every which way at every meal; however, I am no longer in the artichoke-cleaning business. Canned and frozen must suffice.

I have Greek cookbooks which include a dish similar to this, but I am not sure whether the recipe originally came from Greece or whether it was invented in the kitchen of a mayonnaise company. Whatever its origins, it has certainly hit the spot with a lot of people, including me. My friend Maureen Grant adds frozen spinach that has been thawed, squeezed dry and chopped to her artichoke dip. It tastes great. If you choose to include spinach, increase the amount of mayonnaise and Parmesan by 1/2 cup each.

❧

Preheat oven to 375°F.

Mix ingredients, reserving 2 or 3 tablespoons Parmesan cheese. Pour into an oven-to-table baking dish. Sprinkle with reserved Parmesan.

Bake 20 to 25 minutes. Serve warm with thinly sliced French bread or crackers.

Marinated Red and Yellow Peppers

O ne day, while browsing around Litteri's, Washington, D.C.'s wholesale Italian grocer, I found a jar of peppers from Italy called "Sweet and Sour." Intrigued, I bought it. They were so good I went back and bought a case, then another to give to my friends. I began to buy them in gallon-sized cans. But nothing good lasts forever. Somehow my lovely pepper got caught in a tariff dispute between the Common Market and the United States and went into escrow in some warehouse in New Jersey, never to appear again. I have combed markets from here to San Francisco but no luck. Jaded palates must be dealt with, and so, forced into the kitchen, I attempted to duplicate my lovelies.

2 to 3 pounds large red and
    yellow bell peppers

1 cup olive oil

1/4 cup fresh lemon juice

2 cloves garlic, minced (optional)

Salt and freshly ground black
    pepper to taste

- Makes about 2 cups

Grill the peppers on an outdoor grill or under a broiler until skin is blackened and bubbly. Remove and place in a brown paper bag. Close and leave peppers for 15 minutes. Peel and quarter peppers, removing seeds and veins.

    Combine remaining ingredients. Pour over peppers and marinate for at least a day, preferably several. Serve these alone as part of an antipasto platter, or add to salads.

Caviar Mousse

2 tablespoons cold water

1½ teaspoons unflavored gelatin

¾ cup sour cream

¼ cup finely grated onion

3 hard-cooked eggs

¼ cup mayonnaise

4 teaspoons fresh lemon juice

½ teaspoon Worcestershire sauce

1 teaspoon salt

¼ teaspoon freshly ground white pepper

3 drops hot pepper sauce

3 ounces black lumpfish caviar

- Makes about 2 cups

Someone brought this dish to a potluck supper at my home once and I remember thinking, "What a strange dish." It sounded awful, but it was wonderful. This is easy and very elegant to serve as part of a buffet and can be the one appetizer you bring out to impress your in-laws. I like to serve it with smoked salmon on the side for a double dose of elegance.

&

Put water in small bowl. Sprinkle gelatin over water. Put bowl in pan of hot water and stir until gelatin is completely dissolved. Let cool.

Combine remaining ingredients except caviar in food processor. Blend until smooth. Pour in medium bowl and stir in dissolved gelatin. Fold in caviar.

Grease a decorative 2-cup mold. Fill with caviar mixture. Chill until gelatin is set.

Unmold on serving plate by holding a hot towel on the bottom of the mold. If the hot towel doesn't dislodge it, try a bit of prying with a rubber spatula. Garnish with lemon slices and parsley (or smoked salmon). Serve with cocktail breads or crackers.

Soups

AS MY FRIEND Bill McCormick once said, "I never met a soup I didn't like." That's probably not true for all of us, but I'm sure in general we all appreciate a nice hot soup on a cold winter's eve and a nice cold soup on a hot summer's day. Soup is pretty inexpensive to make, and what a comfort food when you don't feel well. My mother always gave me a good homemade chicken noodle soup when I was not well.

The soup pot left simmering on the back of the wood stove years ago was the recipient of an odd assortment of bones and vegetable peelings. The cook had to choose between feeding the vegetable peelings to the chickens or putting them in the pot. The soup pot accepts bits and pieces of just about anything unused or left over. I had a friend who saved uneaten tossed salad and pureed it in the blender the next day to make soup.

Remember to toss a lemon shell into your pot while the soup is simmering, or add a squeeze of lemon juice to your chili, gazpacho or minestrone. Lemon juice in your vichyssoise (potato and leek soup in plain-speak) will make it sparkle. I don't believe there is a soup out there which can't benefit from a little lemon.

Speaking of flavor, always allow your chilled soups to warm up a bit at room temperature before serving. Cold masks the flavor and seasoning of any dish.

Palestine Soup

2 tablespoons unsalted butter

2 medium celery stalks with leaves, chopped

1 medium onion, finely chopped

1 small white potato, peeled and sliced

1 pound Jerusalem artichokes, scrubbed well, cut into 1/4-inch slices

4 cups chicken broth

2 to 3 tablespoons fresh lemon juice

Salt and Lemon Pepper (see recipe page 24) to taste

3/4 teaspoon ground coriander

1/2 cup cream or milk to thin to desired consistency

• Serves 6

I would like one day to write a book on food nomenclature, and most certainly Jerusalem artichokes would qualify for inclusion. These are neither artichokes nor from Jerusalem but are in fact a native American tuber carried back to Europe by Samuel de Champlain. The Europeans took to them in a big way, and we owe most of their uses and recipes to European chefs.

The story of how they came to be called Jerusalem artichokes is rather long to include here. American Indians called them sunroot, and California growers have named them sunchoke. By any name, they are an under-appreciated vegetable. The flavor is smoky, the texture crisp—only the gnarled looks might put you off. Thankfully, the skin is thin like a new potato, and you need only scrub them well before cooking.

❧

Melt butter in heavy saucepan. Sauté celery and onion for 5 minutes over medium heat. Add potato and Jerusalem artichoke. Stir to coat with butter. Add chicken broth, lemon juice, and seasonings. Simmer, partly covered, for 20 to 25 minutes, or until vegetables are soft. Cool. Puree in blender or food processor. Press through sieve. Return to saucepan. Stir in cream or milk. Reheat briefly. Check seasoning.

Cold Curried Carrot Soup

The carrot and curry make a lovely combination of flavors, and the color such a pretty presentation. Curry powder, as you probably know, originated in India, where cooks will grind up to 20 spices, herbs and seeds each day to make their special blend. The curry powder we buy prepared is but a pale imitation. It will usually contain cumin, coriander, fenugreek, turmeric (the yellow color), dill and cardamom. If you don't use curry powder much, buy in small quantities, because the pungency of the spices is quickly lost. As with all spices and herbs, store in a cool, dark place to help retain freshness. You may also serve this soup hot. Pass a bowl of homemade croutons.

Sauté carrots and onion in butter in a heavy saucepan over medium heat. Add curry powder and lemon zest. Cook 3 to 4 minutes, stirring.

Add chicken broth and water. Simmer until carrots are tender, about 15 to 20 minutes. Cool and puree. Add lemon juice to taste. Stir in cream or yogurt. Adjust seasoning.

Refrigerate at least 8 hours to meld flavors. Bring to room temperature before serving.

1 pound carrots, peeled and sliced

1 large onion, chopped

3 tablespoons unsalted butter

1 teaspoon curry powder (mild)

3 strips of lemon zest

1 can condensed chicken broth

1 quart water

Fresh lemon juice to taste

1 cup heavy cream or plain yogurt

Salt and freshly ground black pepper to taste

- Serves 8

Black Bean Soup

1 cup dried black turtle beans or two 14½-ounce cans cooked black beans

2 tablespoons olive oil

1 very large onion, chopped

4 large cloves garlic, chopped

3 cups chicken stock

Ham hock (optional)

Extra water or stock to thin soup

½ cup chopped green bell pepper

1 large tomato, chopped

¼ cup chopped cilantro

2 tablespoons balsamic vinegar

1 tablespoon freshly grated lemon zest

2 tablespoons soy sauce

1½ teaspoons dried oregano

2 teaspoons ground cumin

1 bay leaf

Salt and Lemon Pepper (see recipe page 24) to taste

¼ cup fresh lemon juice

Sour cream or plain yogurt

Fresh cilantro for garnish

- Serves 6

*T*his could be the best black bean soup you have ever tasted. Why, you might ask? It's because of the lemon juice and balsamic vinegar. Who would have thought the day would come when we would be adding Italian vinegar to a Latin soup?

Make this soup a day or so ahead to allow the flavors to meld. You may add sausage or smoked meats for a heartier soup. P.S. If you want soup for an army, double the recipe.

ᔎᔪ

Wash the beans and soak overnight in water 2 inches above the level of the beans. Drain.

In a large, heavy soup pot, sauté onion and garlic in olive oil. Add beans, stock, and the optional ham hock. Bring to a boil and simmer for about 2 hours (½ hour if using canned beans), or until beans are tender. Add water or stock as needed to prevent soup from becoming too thick.

Remove half of bean mixture and puree in a food processor. Return to soup pot. Add green pepper, tomato, cilantro, balsamic vinegar, lemon zest, soy sauce, oregano, cumin, bay leaf, salt, and Lemon Pepper. Simmer another hour or so, adding liquid as needed to keep it nice and soupy.

Add lemon juice. Check seasoning. Top with sour cream or yogurt and fresh cilantro.

Creamy Corn Crab Soup

*T*his soup is so smooth, so creamy, so divine—and so easy. It is one of my favorite soups to serve to company. You may be tempted to omit the straining of the creamed corn mixture, but please restrain yourself and *you will be rewarded*. It is not hard and takes five minutes.

For nirvana, use cream. If your conscience can't take that, use milk, regular or low-fat. Over time, you will learn which one provides the consistency and depth of flavor you prefer. P.S. If you are really back to basics, buy a Lee's fresh–corn cutter/creamer and substitute fresh corn for canned. You'll know real corn heaven, not to mention impress your friends no end.

❧

Sauté onion in butter until tender. Add corn and lemon juice. Cook over low heat, stirring, for 20 minutes. Cool. Puree in food processor. Push through strainer into a heavy, 2-quart saucepan. Add salt and Lemon Pepper.

Add half-and-half and cook over low heat for 15 minutes. Thin with milk or more half-and-half to reach desired consistency. Add crab and cook, stirring gently, until heated. Adjust seasoning. Serve topped with lemon slices and chopped parsley.

1 medium onion

2 tablespoons unsalted butter

A 16-ounce can cream-style corn

2 tablespoons fresh lemon juice, or more, to taste

Salt and Lemon Pepper (see recipe page 24) to taste

2 cups half-and-half

Milk to thin to desired consistency

1/2 pound backfin or lump crabmeat, well picked over

4 thin slices of lemon

Chopped fresh parsley to garnish

- Serves 4

Mrs. Kay's Cold Borscht

1 cucumber, peeled and finely chopped

3 teaspoons kosher salt

1 bottle prepared borscht (I find Mother's brand to my liking)

¼ cup fresh lemon juice

1 to 2 tablespoons granulated sugar (if you find the liquid too tart)

1 egg yolk, lightly beaten

4 or 5 green onions, chopped

Sour cream for garnish

• Serves 4

*T*his recipe was given to me years ago in Hawaii by Lilliana Kay, who is truly a superb cook. Lilliana got the recipe from her mother-in-law, Mrs. Benn Kay of Milwaukee. There are people who make borscht from scratch, but I am not one of them. To justify the extra time it takes, I must see a much greater return in flavor for my efforts. Canned or bottled beets work very well for me, and I think you will find them a worthy substitute.

❧

Salt cucumber with 2 teaspoons of salt and allow to drain in a strainer. Drain borscht juice into 2-quart nonreactive saucepan, reserving beets. Warm liquid in saucepan. Add lemon juice. Taste. Add sugar if you wish.

Beat egg in a small heatproof bowl. Gradually stir in some of the hot liquid, a tablespoon at a time, until egg is warmed. Add back into saucepan, stirring constantly. Heat. *Do not boil.* Cool.

Smush green onions with 1 teaspoon salt in a mortar or bowl. Rinse salt from cucumbers. Add cucumbers, green onions, and reserved, drained beets to soup.

Serve well chilled, with a dollop of sour cream on top of each bowl. Swirl a bit to get the candy-striped look.

Spinach and Avocado Soup

Those old tales of kids sitting at the table for hours because they wouldn't eat their canned spinach are true. Lots of psychosis out there from that, not to mention spinach haters. Today spinach has been reincarnated, probably due to the availability of fresh.

This is an unusual soup, but expand your food horizons. Once you begin thinking anything is possible in the kitchen, you will go on to create your own recipes.

❧

Place spinach, with water still clinging to leaves, in a large nonreactive pot. Cover. Cook for about 5 minutes, until leaves are wilted. Cool. Squeeze the liquid from the spinach and finely chop.

Melt the butter in a heavy saucepan. Stir in spinach, salt, Lemon Pepper, and nutmeg. Add flour. Cook over medium heat, stirring, for a couple of minutes. Add 2 cups milk and chicken broth. Bring to a boil.

Cover and simmer 10 minutes, stirring occasionally. Stir in 1/2 cup cream or milk and season to taste with hot pepper sauce.

Cool. Puree. Add avocados and lemon juice and puree to a smooth texture. Add remaining 1/2 cup cream or milk. Check seasoning. Serve hot or cold, with a dollop of whipped cream or yogurt.

1 pound fresh spinach, stems removed and washed well but not dried

2 tablespoons unsalted butter

Salt and Lemon Pepper (see recipe page 24) to taste

Pinch of nutmeg

3 tablespoons all-purpose flour

2 cups milk (low-fat okay)

2 cups chicken broth

1 cup heavy cream or milk

Dash hot pepper sauce

2 ripe avocados, peeled and cut into chunks

1/3 cup fresh lemon juice

Whipped cream or plain yogurt

- Serves 6

Summer's Day Fruit Soup

1 medium-sized ripe cantaloupe

4 apples, the most flavorful you
    can find, peeled and chopped

1/2 pound seedless green grapes

1 pint fresh strawberries, stems
    removed

6 cups water

1/2 cup granulated sugar

3/4 cup fresh lemon juice

2-inch piece of cinnamon stick

4 whole cloves

1 1/2 cups fresh orange juice

Yogurt and fresh fruit to garnish

- Serves 8

*T*his is so healthy, lovely and refreshing. Almost like a drink in a bowl. I think you will find that most people adore a fruit soup, once they get past the idea. It is unusual. In fact, I can't remember ever being served a fruit soup for lunch in a private home. I hope you will try it and feel free to substitute any fruit you may have on hand, making sure it is perfectly ripe. Add more sugar or even honey if this is too tart for your taste.

ℒℯ

Combine fruits, water, sugar, 1/2 cup lemon juice, and spices in a nonreactive saucepan. Bring to a boil. Reduce heat and partially cover. Simmer 15 minutes. Remove cinnamon stick and cloves.

Put the fruit through a sieve or puree in blender or food processor and then strain. Stir in the remainder of the lemon juice and the orange juice. Chill.

Serve with a dollop of yogurt and fresh fruit to garnish.

Cold Avocado Soup

This lovely green soup, topped with a lemon slice and red caviar, is an eye-catching first course—and it tastes so good. Remember to remove this from the refrigerator half an hour or so before serving. Make sure you have ripe avocados.

❦

Puree avocado, 2 cups chicken broth, lemon juice, chili powder, and coriander in a blender or food processor. Pour into a large, heavy-bottomed, nonreactive saucepan with the remaining 2 cups of chicken broth. Heat for 10 minutes. *Do not boil.* Thin to desired consistency with milk or cream. Add seasoning to taste. Chill.

To serve, ladle into bowls and top each with a lemon slice and a spoonful of caviar.

2 large avocados, peeled and cut into chunks

4 cups chicken broth

2 tablespoons fresh lemon juice

2 teaspoons mild chili powder

1/2 teaspoon ground coriander

2 cups milk or cream to thin soup

Salt and Lemon Pepper (see recipe page 24) to taste

6 lemon slices

Small jar of red caviar

- Serves 6

Avgolemono (Greek Egg-Lemon Soup)

6 cups chicken stock (preferably homemade)

1/3 cup long grain rice or small pasta shapes

1 teaspoon grated lemon zest

3 egg yolks

1/4 cup fresh lemon juice

Salt and freshly ground white pepper to taste

Thinly sliced lemons to garnish

Minced parsley to garnish

- Serves 6

*T*his is pronounced ahv-goh-LEH-moh-noh. If you can learn to pronounce the name you will be very proud of yourself. The Greeks use the name for both a soup and a sauce. Avgolemono is a refreshing, tart, intriguing and, most of all, easy soup to make. I like to make it a day ahead of time to let the flavors mingle and serve at room temperature. Avgolemono can be the first course for your Greek meal, which means of course that you can learn to make and then pronounce the names of even more wonderful Greek dishes made with lemon.

ℰ∂

Bring stock to a boil in large nonreactive saucepan. Add rice or pasta and lemon zest. Simmer about 15 minutes, or until rice or pasta is tender.

Beat egg yolks in a small bowl. Beat in lemon juice. Slowly incorporate small amounts of chicken broth into the yolks, stirring constantly, until yolks are warmed. Pour egg mixture into chicken broth, stirring constantly. Simmer about 5 minutes over low heat, until slightly thickened. Add salt and pepper to taste. Serve with slices of lemon and parsley on top.

Roasted Pumpkin or Butternut Squash Soup

When we lived in Malta, the veggie man came around every morning. No matter what the season, there was always a huge pumpkin-like vegetable on the tailgate of his truck, from which he would hack off any size piece you wanted. When I came back to the United States I continued to make pumpkin or squash soup as soon as the weather began to turn cool. Roasting the vegetables before pureeing intensifies the flavor. When I am in a hurry, though, I will simply throw everything except the cream in a pot, cook and puree, then add the cream.

※

Preheat oven to 375°F.

Toss pumpkin and squash, onions, carrot, garlic, and lemon zest with lemon juice and olive oil. Sprinkle with salt and pepper.

Spray a 15 x 10-inch baking sheet with no-stick cooking spray or line pan with aluminum foil. Spread the vegetables on the baking sheet and bake until tender, about 15 to 20 minutes, stirring once or twice. Be careful not to burn the onions and garlic. Cool. Puree in food processor. Transfer to a large nonreactive soup pot. Add chicken broth, thyme, and nutmeg. Simmer for 30 minutes. Add extra lemon juice. Adjust seasoning. Thin to desired consistency with milk or cream. Warm thoroughly. Serve garnished with chopped green onion.

4 cups pumpkin or butternut squash or a combination, peeled, seeded, and cut in chunks

2 large onions, coarsely chopped

1 carrot, peeled and sliced

2 large cloves garlic, halved

1 tablespoon grated lemon zest

1/4 cup fresh lemon juice

3 tablespoons olive oil

Salt and freshly ground black pepper to taste

5 cups chicken broth

1/2 teaspoon dried thyme

Few grates of fresh nutmeg

1/4 cup fresh chopped parsley

Additional lemon juice to taste (2 to 3 tablespoons should do)

1 to 2 cups milk or cream

2 to 3 green onions, chopped

- Serves 8

Salads

PERHAPS NO OTHER food category offers us the opportunity to create such beautiful and original food offerings. A salad means a mixture, and there are no longer any guidelines for what can and cannot go into a salad, either hot or cold. We now have in our supermarkets wonderful selections of lettuces and other greens and exotic ingredients from other countries.

Salads provide an ideal opportunity to become a kitchen artist by mixing and matching colors, textures and consistencies. Many of the combinations we find listed on restaurant menus we would never have dreamed of eating 10 years ago—or even five. The taste sensations are wonderful, new and exciting. Join the fun and make your own.

The same goes for your salad dressings. You can substitute lemon juice for vinegar in most of your recipes, or use half each. Those on a low-fat diet will find that a squeeze of lemon juice on salad greens and vegetables is a wonderful dressing in and of itself. If allowed, you can add a bit of olive oil. Sometimes the simplest things are the best. A couple of tablespoons of lemon juice will really perk up your standard pasta or rice salad recipes.

The Lemon Garlic Dressing that accompanies the Salad Nicoise recipe is my favorite, but when I want a shortcut I will use a packet of Four Seasons Italian. I prepare it using half lemon juice and half balsamic vinegar and a tablespoon more water than the ready-mix calls for, add a teaspoon or so of Dijon mustard, and shake well. Sometimes I add a bit of fresh garlic. Use Lemon Garlic Dressing to marinate fish, meats and vegetables. You won't be disappointed. I prepare one of my favorite quick salads by marinating any vegetables I have on hand— asparagus is particularly good—in Lemon Garlic Dressing and serving them with some shredded prosciutto and goat cheese. Chicken and tuna rise above their normal humble status with this dressing.

The salads in this section are a cross-section of my personal regulars.

Caesar Salad

2 heads romaine lettuce, torn into bite-size pieces

2 teaspoons crushed or minced garlic

1 teaspoon dry mustard

Few grinds of black pepper

1 teaspoon Worcestershire sauce

A 2-ounce can anchovies, drained and patted dry

1/3 cup fresh lemon juice

1 egg, coddled (boiled for 60 seconds)

1/2 cup grated Parmesan cheese

1/2 cup olive oil

1 cup croutons (sauté 1 cup cubed French bread in 2 tablespoons olive oil) to garnish

- Serves 6 to 8

A Caesar salad is made with anchovies! What confuses me is how many people say they love Caesar salad, but never get it with anchovies. Let's stop the confusion and give the anchovy-less salad another name. Before including this recipe in the book, I debated a bit and then took an informal poll to determine people's favorite salad and how often they prepare it. The answer was Caesar, but most people said they used bottled Caesar dressing or only ate it when dining out. So I decided it was my duty to give everyone a good recipe to make for company and to encourage people to do right by their favorite salad.

જ્ઞ

Place all ingredients except lettuce, olive oil, and croutons in food processor. With food processor running, slowly add olive oil. Toss dressing with lettuce. Garnish with croutons. Offer extra freshly ground black pepper to taste.

Simple Salad

The following is made with red or green leaf lettuce, the kind you can even grow yourself. You may substitute other varieties of lettuce, but the one thing you should do is shred by hand. This will intensify the flavor. Proportions are approximate and based on a medium head of lettuce. You can make this a couple of hours in advance of serving. Please do add enough Parmesan to suit yourself.

❧

Toss the lettuce with the lemon juice and vinegar. Add Parmesan cheese. Toss again. Add salt and pepper. Taste and adjust seasoning.

1 head red or green leaf lettuce, washed, dried, and coarsely shredded by hand

3 tablespoons lemon juice

2 tablespoons good balsamic vinegar

1/4 to 1/2 cup grated Parmesan cheese (or more to taste)

Salt and freshly ground black pepper to taste

● Serves 8

Salad Niçoise

2 pounds red potatoes, steamed and sliced

1 large red onion, sliced

1 or 2 cans of water-packed tuna, drained

Salad greens

2 cups whole green beans, cooked

1 cup black olives, preferably oil-cured

1/2 pint cherry tomatoes or 1 large tomato, cut in wedges

3 hard-cooked eggs, quartered

1 green bell pepper, cut in rings

1/2 cup roasted red bell pepper, cut in strips (see Marinated Red and Yellow Peppers page 49 or use bottled Italian or Spanish)

1 can rolled anchovies with capers

Salt and freshly ground black pepper to taste

• Serves 8

I first encountered what has become my signature summer luncheon dish on "the trip to Europe" at the tender age of 23. *Niçoise* translated means "as prepared in Nice"; dishes with niçoise in their titles will include tomatoes, black olives, garlic and anchovies. Salad Niçoise also includes hard-cooked eggs, tuna, green beans, onions and, in my case, potatoes.

This is a composed salad, built from the bottom. The juxtaposition of all the colorful ingredients makes a nice presentation. I suggest you dress the salad lightly and serve with extra dressing on the side.

You may put this salad together at the last minute, but, if you have time, marinate the tuna, onion and potatoes in some of the dressing for an hour or two before assembling the salad. To make the most awesome potato salad, slice your cooked potatoes while still hot and toss with some of the lemon dressing before adding mayonnaise. The potatoes will absorb the dressing. *Magnifique!*

෩

Prepare the Lemon Garlic Dressing (see below). Combine potatoes and onion with 1/2 cup of dressing. Marinate for an hour or two at room temperature, stirring occasionally. Put the drained tuna in a small bowl and pour a small amount of dressing on top. Marinate

70

for an hour or two at room temperature.

Line a large salad or serving bowl (preferably with angled sides to display all the pretty ingredients) with greens. Drain potatoes and onion, reserving dressing. Arrange potatoes and onion on top of greens. Put tuna in the middle. Arrange the rest of the ingredients around the tuna and on top of the potatoes and onion.

Drizzle with the reserved dressing used to marinate potatoes and onions and add more dressing if you wish. Serve additional dressing on the side.

Lemon Garlic Dressing
Combine all ingredients.

LEMON GARLIC DRESSING

2 cups olive oil

1/2 cup tarragon wine vinegar

1/4 cup fresh lemon juice

2 or 3 large cloves garlic, crushed

1 tablespoon dried mustard

1 teaspoon granulated sugar

1 tablespoon salt

Freshly ground black pepper to taste

- Makes 2 3/4 cups

Panzanella (Tomato-Bread Salad)

4 cups peeled, seeded, and diced ripe tomatoes

10 ounces stale (2 to 3 days old) Italian bread, whirled in food processor to make bread crumbs

1 teaspoon crushed or minced garlic

1 cup minced red onion

1 cup shredded, packed fresh basil

¼ cup olive oil

2 tablespoons fresh lemon juice

1 tablespoon balsamic vinegar

Salt and freshly ground black pepper to taste

• Serves 8

*E*very time I serve this, people request the recipe. Since it must be made with summer-ripe tomatoes, it is a good dish to serve at an outdoor barbecue. Try to make the salad early in the day to allow the flavors to mingle, but it is not the end of the world if you don't have time to do this. The object is to have the bread absorb the juice from the tomatoes, become soft and blend in with the other ingredients. You can garnish with anchovies and black olives.

৪৯

Put tomatoes in a nonreactive colander to drain. Mix tomatoes, bread crumbs, garlic, onion, basil, olive oil, lemon juice, balsamic vinegar, and salt and pepper.

Allow to stand for at least 30 minutes, preferably 45. Mix well, making sure the bread is thoroughly incorporated. Check for seasoning. Serve at room temperature.

Couscous Salad

My husband was once a Naval attaché in Morocco. He grew to love many Moroccan dishes, particularly couscous when served with a slightly spicy lamb stew. Couscous is a wonderful, versatile grain alternative that has found favor, given the new emphasis on complex carbohydrates in our diet. I love it fixed so many ways—plain, using a meat or vegetable broth as the liquid; topped with vegetables, beans, meat stews or poached chicken; or even as a sweet dessert. I particularly like it made spicy with Harissa sauce (red chili peppers, coriander, cumin and garlic). In this recipe, the couscous grain is swollen using chicken broth and lemon juice. This salad is best made a day in advance of serving. It keeps well. I serve it a lot in the summer with cold chicken, lamb or fish. It is light, lovely and very good for you!

ৡৡ

Bring broth to a boil. Add lemon juice and couscous. Cover and remove from heat. Let stand until the liquid is absorbed, about 5 minutes. Season to taste with salt and pepper. Stir in remaining ingredients. Serve at room temperature.

1½ cups chicken or vegetable broth

½ cup fresh lemon juice

1½ cups uncooked couscous

Salt and freshly ground black pepper to taste

1 teaspoon ground cumin

½ teaspoon grated lemon zest

1 clove garlic, minced

½ cup minced flat-leaf parsley

½ cup thinly sliced green onions

½ cup chopped red or green bell pepper

½ cup finely shredded carrot

½ cup seeded and chopped tomato

¼ cup olive oil

• Serves 6

Greek Salad

1 large tomato, cut into 8 pieces

1 small cucumber, peeled and chopped

2 to 3 ounces feta cheese, in chunks

10 oil-cured black olives

2 tablespoons extra-virgin olive oil

1 tablespoon fresh lemon juice

Pinch or two of dried oregano

Salt and freshly ground black pepper to taste (remember, the feta will be salty)

- Serves 2

I have seen so many versions of Greek salad that I almost believe people think it can contain anything in the refrigerator. I have spent a lot of time in Greece, and the ingredients listed below are what I have been served when I ordered a Greek salad in a taverna or when eating in a friend's home.

Please do not make this salad in the dead of winter! It cries out for the ripest, freshest tomatoes and cucumbers. As for the feta, visit your local Greek or Mediterranean market, where you may find Greek, Bulgarian or Turkish feta. The Turkish is usually a bit saltier, but delicious.

ॐ

Divide tomato, cucumber, feta cheese, and olives between two plates. Sprinkle with remaining ingredients.

Tzatziki (Cucumber and Yogurt Salad)

Tzatziki is part of the Greek *mezedhes* (mixed appetizers) platter. This dish is served throughout the Middle East as well as in Greece. It is very refreshing, particularly when served with spicy foods. I usually serve it as an accompaniment to spicy lamb couscous.

Find the best plain yogurt you can (usually in a health food store). For years I drained yogurt using cheesecloth in a strainer; now they make conical yogurt strainers with plastic mesh. I could wish for a bit larger size, but anything that eliminates the cheesecloth mess is okay with me. Drained yogurt becomes yogurt cheese, which can substitute for cream cheese, mayonnaise, sour cream and even butter in some cases. A most useful product, particularly for those of you on a fat-free diet. Salting the cucumbers helps pull out their moisture so that your salad does not become watery.

Drain yogurt for at least 2 hours. Sprinkle salt on cucumbers and drain in colander for about 30 minutes. Rinse off salt and drain thoroughly. Combine all ingredients. Let sit for at least 2 hours to allow flavors to meld.

2 cups plain yogurt

2 cucumbers, peeled and shredded

2 teaspoons salt

1 tablespoon fresh lemon juice

2 cloves garlic, minced

1 tablespoon olive oil

1 teaspoon grated lemon zest

Salt and freshly ground black pepper to taste

- Serves 6 to 8

Salmon Mousse

2 cups cooked salmon or a
  14½-ounce can

¼ cup water or, if using canned
  salmon, ¼ cup juice from
  the can

2 tablespoons fresh lemon juice

1 envelope unflavored gelatin

½ cup boiling water

1 small onion, cut into pieces

1 cup plain yogurt

½ cup mayonnaise

½ cup fresh dill leaves, snipped

½ teaspoon paprika

1 teaspoon salt

¼ teaspoon hot pepper sauce, or
  to taste

Lettuce leaves (optional)

Lemon slices

¼ pound smoked salmon
  (optional)

- Serves 6

Now don't let the word *mousse* frighten you off. A mousse is so easy to make and almost foolproof. This recipe is particularly easy, since it is made entirely in the food processor.

For years I made this mousse with heavy cream and full-fat mayonnaise; while this dish is not as creamy and rich, the yogurt gives it a nice tang. I usually serve this as part of my buffet table or when I have dieting friends over for a light summer lunch. You may use leftover poached salmon or canned red salmon.

୧ର

If using canned salmon, remove the dark skin. Put the water or salmon juice, lemon juice, and gelatin in food processor. Add boiling water. Process 1 minute. Add onion, salmon, yogurt, mayonnaise, dill, paprika, and salt. Process until smooth. Taste for seasoning. Add hot pepper sauce to taste.

Pour mixture into a greased 4-cup mold. Refrigerate until firm, 2 to 3 hours. Unmold onto a plate, covered with lettuce if you wish. Garnish with lemon slices.

Note: If using smoked salmon, pour half of the mousse mixture into your mold, arrange half a cup of chopped smoked salmon on top, then pour in the remainder of the mousse mixture. You can top with more strips of smoked salmon after unmolding.

Addictive Cucumber Salad

In my summers growing up, my mother made lots of cucumber salad, marinating the cucumbers in white vinegar, sugar and onion and sometimes adding sour cream or fresh dill. Recently, when my friend Prudence Squier had a bumper crop of English cukes (the long, burpless variety), I remembered the dish of my childhood. I fiddled with the ingredients a bit, used seasoned rice wine vinegar (available in Oriental grocery stores and many supermarkets), added lemon juice—and loved it. The result is below, and I dare you to have one cucumber slice and not eat more. These cucumbers are nice to serve with sandwiches and on a buffet table.

૭ә

Slice cucumber into thin slices. Put in a nonreactive strainer and toss with salt. Let stand an hour or so to draw off excess moisture. Rinse with cold water. Drain well or pat dry with towel. Put in a bowl and toss with remaining ingredients. The salad will keep for weeks in the refrigerator.

1 long, thin English or hothouse cucumber

1 tablespoon salt

1/2 cup seasoned rice wine vinegar

1/2 medium-sized onion, thinly sliced

1/2 cup fresh dill, snipped

3 tablespoons fresh lemon juice

Salt and freshly ground black pepper to taste

- Makes 2 cups

Melitzanes (Eggplant Salad)

2 medium eggplants, purple, shiny, and soft to the touch

2 tablespoons fresh lemon juice

1/4 cup finely chopped onion

2 tablespoons extra-virgin olive oil

1 tomato, peeled, seeded, and diced

1/2 teaspoon salt

Lemon Pepper (see recipe page 24) to taste

Oil-cured black olives for garnish

• Serves 4

ifferent versions of this dish can be found in Greece, Turkey and most Middle Eastern countries. I love it but usually make it only in the summer, when I can blister the eggplant on the outside grill to get the perfect roasted flavor. You can, however, bake it in the oven or use a stove-top grill. Serve in a nice bowl, surrounded by black olives and pieces of warm pita bread for scooping.

🙩

Bake or grill the eggplant until it is soft to the touch and the skin wrinkled. Cool. Peel. Cut in half lengthwise and discard the seeds. Mash the eggplant. Sprinkle with lemon juice.

Sauté onion in olive oil until tender. Combine eggplant, onion, tomatoes, salt, and Lemon Pepper. Serve with black olives and pita bread.

Lemon Fennel Salad

ennel always makes me think of the sunny Mediterranean, where it is grown extensively in the countries that rim the shores. The Italians in particular make good use of this vegetable. If you don't know fennel, it is that green bulb with tall, feathery foliage. The texture is crunchy like celery, and the flavor has a mere hint of anise, but sweeter and more delicate. When cooked, there is an ever-so-slight anise aroma. Serve this when next you have an outdoor cook-out. I think it will please your family and guests.

❧

Slice each fennel bulb into thin lengthwise slices. Blanch slices in boiling salted water until crisp-tender, 2 to 3 minutes. Drain and cool.

Combine fennel strips, onion, Lemon Garlic Dressing, salt, and Lemon Pepper. Marinate 1 hour at room temperature. Check for seasoning. Serve on bed of greens, garnished with tomatoes and chopped cilantro.

4 fennel bulbs, trimmed of the tough outer layer and strings

1 red onion, thinly sliced

1/4 cup fresh lemon juice

1/2 cup Lemon Garlic Dressing (see recipe page 71)

Salt and Lemon Pepper (see recipe page 24) to taste

Assorted greens

3 tomatoes cut in wedges to garnish

2 to 3 tablespoons finely chopped cilantro

• Serves 6

Entrees

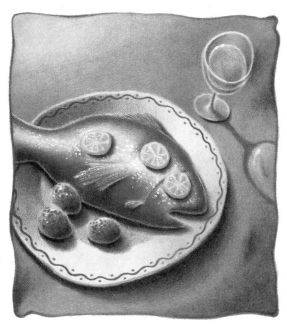

IN THE UNITED States, *entree* means the main course, and in years past it consisted of a fish or meat or poultry dish, served with potatoes or starch of some sort, vegetables and perhaps a salad. Pizza would never have qualified. Anything goes now, but for organizational purposes I have retained the category and expanded it a bit. In deciding what to include, I wanted to keep the recipes simple and not too time-consuming. But I had to share a few of my more elaborate favorites, such as lamb shanks and one or two out-of-the-ordinary dishes to pique your interest. My son Blair prevailed upon me to include some of his favorite lemon pasta dishes. After scrambled eggs he learned to make spaghetti, and to this day his preference is for simple pastas, often tossed with nothing but butter and cheese. It was his idea years ago to put lemon in the homemade pasta dough. Now you see it ready-made in the supermarket.

If you have ever visited the summer places of the Mediterranean, you may recall that main courses—no matter fish or meat—are usually accompanied by lemon on the plate. In fact, the local patrons seem to squeeze lemon on everything. Do they have more educated palates than we Americans, or do they know something about healthy eating habits that we might consider emulating?

Baked Monkfish

A 2-pound fillet of monkfish, skinned

3 cloves garlic, slivered

1/3 cup olive oil

Enough leaf tops from a fennel bulb to line a glass baking dish

1/3 cup fresh lemon juice

3 or 4 green onions, sliced

Salt and freshly ground black pepper to taste

3 or 4 sprigs of fresh lemon thyme or thyme or 1/2 teaspoon dried thyme

1 bay leaf

1 lemon, thinly sliced

• Serves 4

Monkfish has been called "the poor man's lobster," and that is not because it's as ugly as a lobster (which it is). The taste and texture are lobster-like, with a wonderful mild, sweet, slightly chewy taste. You can substitute monkfish (also called lotte or anglerfish) in many dishes that call for pieces of lobster. This is one of my favorite ways to prepare monkfish—even my French friends like it.

❧

Preheat oven to 400°F. Dry the monkfish. Stick pieces of slivered garlic into the flesh of the fish. Roll the fish lengthwise and tie with kitchen string. Pour oil into an oval gratin dish large enough to hold the fish comfortably.

Arrange the fennel tops in the dish and place the monkfish on top. Pour lemon juice over fish. Sprinkle with green onions. Season with salt and pepper. Add thyme and bay leaf. Bake for about 20 minutes, or until monkfish is firm. Cover with lemon slices and serve.

Scallops So Simple

To repeat myself, sometimes the simplest things are the best. Not only is this dish plain, it is lightning fast. It can be very elegant as well, if you need a company dinner in a hurry. You can add a few green onions, some parsley and olive oil or butter and serve it over hot spaghetti. That same spaghetti is good served as a cold salad for a light lunch.

You may use tiny bay scallops, which are very sweet and often less expensive than the larger, stronger flavored deep-sea scallops. Judge your cooking time by the size of the scallops.

The Lemon Tartar Sauce recipe included here takes only minutes to make, and it is so much better than the ready-made. The sauce will not keep more than five days in the refrigerator.

❧

Spray a nonstick frying pan with no-stick cooking spray. Sauté scallops over high heat, stirring, until just cooked through, about 1 minute for bay scallops and 3 to 5 minutes for sea scallops. Add lemon juice, salt, and Lemon Pepper, stirring to scrape up bits from the pan. Serve immediately with Lemon Tartar Sauce.

Lemon Tartar Sauce

Whisk olive oil and lemon juice into mayonnaise. Stir in remaining ingredients.

1 pound scallops, rinsed and patted dry with paper towels

Juice from 1 lemon

Salt and Lemon Pepper (see recipe page 24) to taste

- Serves 4

LEMON TARTAR SAUCE

1 tablespoon olive oil

2 tablespoons fresh lemon juice

1/2 cup mayonnaise (regular or low-fat)

2 tablespoons finely minced dill pickle

2 tablespoons finely minced green onion

1 tablespoon finely minced red pimiento

1/2 tablespoon minced capers

1/2 teaspoon freshly grated lemon zest

Salt and freshly ground black pepper to taste

- Makes about 3/4 cup

85

Baked Whole Salmon

A 7- to 8-pound salmon, left whole, with or without the head, cleaned

1/4 cup dry white wine or dry white vermouth

1/2 cup fresh lemon juice

A few sprigs each of fresh basil, thyme, tarragon, rosemary, and parsley, or 1/4 to 1/2 teaspoon of each herb dried

1 large or 2 small bay leaves, crumbled

Small stalk of celery with leaves, chopped

1 carrot, shredded

1 small onion, thinly sliced

2 lemons, thinly sliced

Salt and freshly ground black pepper to taste

1 or 2 English or hothouse cucumbers, thinly sliced

- Serves 10

*P*lease don't be frightened at the thought of cooking a whole fish. It is not difficult, and the fish looks so elegant when it's presented. My fish poacher has been rusting on the storage shelf in the basement since this recipe came into my life. Stuffing the fish cavity with foil before cooking allows you to stand the fish on its tummy on the serving platter. No longer do you have to turn the salmon to get at the meat on the bottom. This dish makes a stunning platter on the buffet table.

If your salmon is smaller than the size called for in the recipe, decrease the cooking time proportionally. You should allow about 3/4 pound per person if the salmon is the main course, a little under half a pound if the fish is part of a buffet dinner.

❧

Preheat oven to 375°F.

Dry the salmon with paper towels. Put the wine and remaining ingredients except fresh lemon slices, salt, pepper, and cucumber in a saucepan and simmer for half an hour or so. Place the fish, positioned on its back (or spine) on a large, heavy-duty piece of aluminum foil. Brace on either side, if necessary, until you fill the cavity. Sprinkle the inside of the fish with salt and pepper. Spoon the wine mixture into the cavity, making sure to evenly distribute the herbs and vegetables. Place the

with Green Sauce and Spicy Mango Salsa

lemon slices around the inside of the cavity. Crumble enough aluminum foil to fill the remaining space and stuff into the cavity. Turn the fish over so that it rests on the foil-stuffed cavity. Bring the bottom foil up to completely enclose the fish, crimping foil to seal the edges tightly. Put the fish in a baking pan.

Bake until the flesh of the fish flakes when you insert a fork, about 1 1/2 hours. Remove from oven. Keeping fish upright, carefully transfer it to a serving platter. Let cool a bit before carefully removing the skin.

Arrange cucumber slices over the fish to resemble fish scales. Place lettuce around the platter. Serve with Green Sauce and Spicy Mango Salsa.

Note: If you are really feeling fancy, fill artichoke bottoms with petit pois (small peas) and place around the fish. I also cut pieces of red pimiento to drape here and there for some nice color.

Green Sauce

This is a pretty green sauce to serve with any baked, poached or grilled fish. Try to make this a few hours in advance of serving.

Whisk olive oil and lemon juice into mayonnaise. Add the remaining ingredients. If you are serving the sauce

GREEN SAUCE

1/3 cup extra-virgin olive oil

1/3 cup fresh lemon juice

1 cup mayonnaise (regular or nonfat)

1/4 cup minced green onions

2 cloves garlic, crushed or finely chopped

2 tablespoons minced fresh dill or tarragon

2 tablespoons snipped fresh chives

1 teaspoon salt

Freshly ground black pepper to taste

- Makes about 2 cups

SPICY MANGO SALSA

1 ripe mango, coarsely chopped

1/2 teaspoon finely minced
jalapeño pepper

2 tablespoons minced cilantro

2 tablespoons finely minced red
onion

2 tablespoons fresh lime juice

1 tablespoon fresh lemon juice

Salt and Lemon Pepper (see
recipe page 24) to taste

● Makes about 1 cup

with a very delicate fish such as sole, omit the garlic.

Spicy Mango Salsa

I first encountered the lovely, luscious mango as a young bride in Hawaii. Later, awaiting the birth of my son Blair, I ate them constantly. As with lemons, mangoes originated in India and form the basis for Major Gray's chutney. In India, both green and ripe mangoes are used extensively in entrees and condiments. This recipe goes well with fish, poached or grilled; cold meats; and as a side dish with pasta, rice or grain salads. Adjust the amount of jalapeño pepper to suit your tolerance level. Wear rubber gloves when playing with jalapeño and keep the fumes far away from your eyes.

Combine all ingredients. Serve only slightly chilled. It will keep 4 to 5 days in the refrigerator.

Aegean Shrimp

This dish goes by many names: Greek Shrimp, Shrimp Scorpio, Shrimp Feta. By any name it is one of my favorite dishes. The combination of shrimp, fresh tomatoes and feta is made in heaven. In the Mediterranean, the dish would be prepared using unpeeled shrimp, with the heads still attached. The taste is better and the shrimp more tender when the shells are left on. It is, however, messy to eat, so this executive decision is up to you. This is worth making a special trip to your local specialty market to get some really first-rate feta. Be sure to serve with lots of good bread to sop up the sauce. Serve with Greek Salad (see recipe page 74) for a very special meal.

❧

Preheat oven to 375°F. In a large sauté pan sauté onion in olive oil over medium-high heat until tender. Stir in tomatoes, garlic, bay leaf, oregano, parsley, and Lemon Pepper. Cook over medium heat for about 10 minutes.

Add shrimp and cook 1 to 2 minutes. Pour mixture into a 1 1/2-quart casserole. (I use a Pyrex pie plate.) Sprinkle with feta. Pour lemon juice over all. Bake 10 to 15 minutes, until heated through and feta is partially melted. Remove from oven. Check seasoning. The need for salt will be determined by the saltiness of the feta.

2 cups chopped onion

1/2 cup olive oil

6 to 8 medium tomatoes, coarsely chopped

2 large cloves garlic, minced

1 bay leaf

1 to 2 teaspoons dried oregano

1/3 cup chopped fresh parsley

Lemon Pepper (see recipe page 24) to taste

1 pound large shrimp, peeled or unpeeled

1/2 pound feta cheese

1/4 cup fresh lemon juice

Salt to taste

- Serves 6

Breaded Lemon Chicken Breasts

6 boneless chicken breast halves

1/3 cup fresh lemon juice

1/2 cup all-purpose flour

Salt and freshly ground black pepper to taste

2 eggs

2 tablespoons water

1 1/4 cups Italian-flavored bread crumbs

1/2 cup grated Parmesan cheese

1 tablespoon grated lemon zest

2 to 3 tablespoons unsalted butter

2 to 3 tablespoons olive oil

Lemon slices

Chopped fresh parsley for garnish

- Serves 6

For years I have pounded chicken breasts and used them in place of veal in many recipes. The chicken breasts are so much cheaper in price, and, to be honest, I don't much miss the veal, except in scallopini. I like to marinate these chicken breasts in lemon juice before breading them, but if you are short of time, just mix a bit of lemon juice in with the egg mixture instead of water. I love to serve an anchovy or two on top of each chicken breast, but then I love anchovies!

ℒ♪

Place each chicken breast half between sheets of wax paper. Pound with a meat pounder until thin. Put in a glass dish with lemon juice, coating each piece. Let stand for a few minutes, no more than 15.

Mix flour, salt, and pepper in a pie plate. Beat eggs and water together in a shallow bowl. Combine bread crumbs, Parmesan cheese, and lemon zest in another pie plate or dish. Remove chicken from lemon juice and dip each breast first in flour mixture, then in egg mixture, and then into bread crumbs, coating well. Shake gently to remove excess. *Recipe can be prepared up to this point in advance. Refrigerate until ready to cook.*

Heat 2 tablespoons butter and add 2 tablespoons olive oil in a large skillet over medium-high heat. Working in batches, sauté the chicken until nicely browned, about 2 minutes per side. *Do not overcook.* Add more butter and oil as needed. Do not crowd skillet. Serve topped with lemon slices and sprinkled with parsley.

Note: If you want to avoid cooking in oil, try the following variation: Pound the chicken breasts, marinate in Lemon Garlic Dressing (see recipe page 71) or bottled Italian or Caesar salad dressing (regular or nonfat) for half an hour, roll in seasoned bread crumbs, and bake at 450°F for 10 minutes, turning once.

Greek Lemon-Pepper Chicken

1/2 cup lemon juice

5 large cloves garlic, chopped

2/3 cup olive oil

2 small chickens, 2 to 3 pounds each, cleaned well and quartered

8 sprigs lemon thyme or regular thyme or 2 tablespoons dried thyme

1 large onion, sliced

Salt to taste

4 teaspoons freshly ground black pepper, or more if you can handle it

1/4 cup grated lemon zest

- Serves 6 to 8

The taste of this chicken dish brings back for me a vivid memory of driving with Greek friends from Athens to their artichoke farm in Iria on the Peloponnesus. We stopped at a seaside taverna for a bite to eat. I can still taste the chicken, potatoes and Greek salad, served at a simple wooden table in the open, with the sound and smell of the seaside.

Use the smallest chicken you can find. Unfortunately, it is very difficult to find what Europeans call a *petit poussin* (small chicken) in the United States. This bird is bigger than our Cornish game hens but smaller than the usual whole chickens you find in the supermarket. Make extra and use the leftover chicken for an incredibly tasty chicken salad. You may roast potatoes in the pan along with the chicken.

❧

Preheat oven to 375°F. Whisk lemon juice, garlic, and olive oil together. Put chicken in a glass dish and pierce the skin a few times with a fork. Pour mixture over chicken. Add thyme and onion slices. Marinate in refrigerator for 2 hours, turning occasionally.

Arrange chicken in roasting pan, skin side up. Pour marinade over top. Sprinkle with salt, pepper, and lemon zest. Bake, basting occasionally, for 1 hour, or until an instant-read meat thermometer reads 180°F. The juices should run clear when pierced with a knife.

Leslie's Chicken

This recipe was given to me by Leslie Freedman when we lived in Malta. Whenever the official social schedule permitted during the two-month island winters, Leslie used to make up a big batch of his chicken to warm our bones.

Get the smallest chicken you can find. Allow about 3/4 pound of chicken per person. If you are allergic to monosodium glutamate, leave out the Accent. The marinade makes a great sauce to serve over steamed rice.

৪৯

Make a paste of salt and garlic by mashing in a mortar or bowl. Combine soy sauce, lemon juice, Accent, sambal oelek, and sugar. Add to garlic paste.

Place chicken in a glass bowl. Pierce chicken in several places with a meat fork. Pour marinade on top. Marinate for about 3 hours in the refrigerator, turning occasionally. Bring to room temperature.

Preheat oven to 375°F. Remove chicken from marinade, reserving marinade, and put in baking pan with butter. Bake 15 minutes. Pour half of marinade over chicken and baste well. Bake about 30 minutes more. Add remaining marinade. Baste again. Bake 15 minutes more. Serve hot over steamed white rice.

2 teaspoons salt

4 large cloves garlic, minced

1 tablespoon Tamari soy sauce

1/4 cup fresh lemon juice

1 teaspoon Accent

1 tablespoon sambal oelek
  (Indonesian red chili paste)

3 tablespoons granulated sugar

1 small chicken, 2 to 3 pounds
  maximum, quartered

8 tablespoons (1 stick) unsalted
  butter

• Serves 2 to 3

Braised Lamb Shanks

1 tablespoon olive oil, more if
needed

4 lamb shanks, 3/4 to 1 pound
each, trimmed

2 tablespoons ground cumin

4 cloves garlic, finely minced or
put through a garlic press

Salt and freshly ground black
pepper to taste

1 cup chicken broth

1/4 cup fresh lemon juice

1 tablespoon grated lemon zest

1 large onion, sliced

1 bay leaf

• Serves 4

*T*his lamb recipe calls for top-of-the-stove braising to the "fall-off-the-bone" stage. Lamb
shanks have become fashionable, and that is
certainly reflected in their price. But I still buy them. I
like this recipe with cumin, but you can use whatever
herbs you like—thyme, rosemary, oregano, tarragon or
herbes de Provence. I once made three versions of this
dish using different seasonings and served them to a
most discerning group of my friends. The one with
cumin was preferred.

I like to serve this with *colcannon* (an Irish dish made
with mashed potatoes, chopped onions and cabbage).
Delicious peasant food at its best. Plain mashed potatoes, noodles, couscous or rice are equally good as
accompaniments.

৪১

Heat olive oil over medium heat in a heavy sauté pan
large enough to hold 4 lamb shanks comfortably without crowding. Brown the lamb shanks on all sides.
Sprinkle shanks with cumin, garlic, salt, and pepper.
Cook for 3 to 4 minutes. Add chicken broth, lemon
juice, lemon zest, onion, and bay leaf.

Simmer, covered, turning occasionally, for about 1 1/2
hours, until the lamb has pulled away from the bone
and is meltingly tender.

Butterflied Leg of Lamb

You haven't lived until you have had spit-roasted lamb, basted with lemon, olive oil and fresh herbs, as they cook it in the Mediterranean, particularly in Greece and Turkey. Lacking a spit, I like to grill a butterflied leg of lamb when I have company in the summer. When the bone is removed, you are left with different thicknesses of meat, so that the cooked leg offers rare, medium-rare and well done. Supermarkets now routinely sell boneless leg of lamb. If you are using fresh herbs, allow the meat to marinate overnight in the refrigerator. With dried herbs, the flavor is more intense, and you won't need to marinate as long.

❧

Crush the garlic, salt, and lemon zest together with a mortar and pestle or with the back of a spoon. Combine with black pepper, olive oil, and herbs. Mix well. Rub on all sides of the leg of lamb. Put in a resealable plastic bag or glass dish, together with onions. Marinate in refrigerator overnight, if possible, or as long as your time permits. Preheat the outdoor grill.

Remove lamb from marinade and allow it to come to room temperature. Add lemon juice to the marinade. Grill lamb, basting with the marinade, about 15 to 20 minutes per side, or until an instant-read meat thermometer registers 140°F in the thickest portion (for rare meat). Let meat rest for about 10 minutes before carving.

5 cloves garlic, minced

2 tablespoons coarse sea salt or kosher salt

3 tablespoons freshly grated lemon zest

1 teaspoon freshly ground black pepper

1/2 cup olive oil

1/4 cup fresh rosemary, lemon thyme, or oregano, or combination, or 4 teaspoons dried herbs

2 onions, chopped

A 6-pound boneless, butterflied leg of lamb, trimmed of membranes and fat

1/2 cup fresh lemon juice

- Serves 6 to 8

Pork Tenderloin Oriental

¹/₂ cup fresh lemon juice

¹/₃ cup soy sauce

¹/₄ cup honey

1 small onion, coarsely chopped

3 large cloves garlic, chopped

1 teaspoon salt

1 teaspoon freshly ground black
    pepper

¹/₂ teaspoon dry mustard

2 teaspoons chopped fresh ginger
    or ¹/₄ teaspoon ground dried
    ginger

1 teaspoon Tiger Sauce (found
    in oriental section of super-
    market) or red chili sauce

2 pork tenderloins, 1 to 2
    pounds each

- Serves 4 to 6

I grew up in hog country when pigs were often corn-fed or fed the potato peelings from the kitchen. Very tasty indeed, but also a bit fatty. Breeders have now succeeded in doing away with much of the fat (and some would say with a lot of the flavor). The tenderloin of pork has little fat to begin with. The marinade has a nice oriental twist that gives the meat a wonderful flavor.

❦

Mix all ingredients except tenderloins. Put the tenderloins in a glass bowl or a large resealable plastic bag. Pour in the marinade. Marinate in refrigerator for several hours or overnight.

Remove pork from marinade, reserving marinade, and bring meat to room temperature before cooking. Cut into 1-inch-thick slices. Preheat the grill. Grill pork over low to medium coals, basting constantly with the marinade, until nicely browned. This should take about 3 to 5 minutes per side. Note that meat brought to room temperature will take less time to cook than meat cooked immediately after it is removed from the refrigerator.

Braised Pork with Lemon

I picked up this recipe when visiting friends in Cascais, Portugal, years ago. I found it most interesting then and still do. My friends Melissa and Rodion Cantacuzene served there at the Embassy and have a great fondness for the food of Portugal, which is not spicy but makes use of lots of fresh herbs. Pork is often overlooked as a choice for stews and braising, but it absorbs flavors very well. Serve this with some nice boiled potatoes and lots of bread to mop up the sauce.

ॐ

Mix onion, lemon juice, wine, and garlic. Add pork cubes and put mixture in a resealable plastic bag. Marinate in refrigerator overnight.

Bring to room temperature. Remove pork from marinade, reserving marinade. Pat meat dry. In a large sauté pan heat olive oil over medium-high heat and sear pork on both sides. Pour off fat from pan and add marinade, cumin, coriander seeds, salt, and pepper. Cover and cook over medium heat for about 45 minutes, stirring occasionally. Add lemon slices. Cover and continue to cook for another 30 minutes, or until pork is nice and tender. Check seasoning. Remove meat to a serving platter. Deglaze the pan with a bit of white wine and pour over meat.

1 medium onion, thinly sliced

1/4 cup fresh lemon juice

1/2 cup dry white wine

3 cloves garlic, chopped

A 2 1/2-pound boneless shoulder or loin of pork, cut into 1 1/2-inch cubes

About 1/4 cup olive oil

1 1/2 teaspoons ground cumin

1 1/2 teaspoons coriander seeds

Salt and freshly ground black pepper to taste

1 lemon, thinly sliced

White wine for deglazing pan

• Serves 6

Lemon Veal Roast

A 6-pound boneless veal shoulder
roast, trimmed and tied

6 cloves garlic, crushed or finely
minced

1/2 cup fresh lemon juice

1/4 cup tarragon wine vinegar

1 1/2 teaspoons dried thyme

1 teaspoon dried oregano

1 teaspoon salt

1 teaspoon freshly ground black
pepper

2/3 cup olive oil

6 potatoes, halved

1 head of garlic (not clove, but
the whole head)

1 cup mayonnaise

• Serves 6 to 8

*T*his roast has, without a doubt, the most divine flavor of any veal dish I have ever tasted. If you are lucky enough to find a rolled veal roast at a reasonable price, grab it and run home and make this for your most special friends. Don't even think of not making the garlic mayonnaise to serve with the roast.

৯৯

Put veal roast in a large, resealable plastic bag. In a bowl whisk together garlic, lemon juice, vinegar, herbs, salt, and pepper. Add olive oil, mixing well. Pour over veal roast. Marinate 2 hours at room temperature or overnight in the refrigerator. Bring to room temperature before roasting. Preheat oven to 350°F.

Remove roast from marinade, reserving marinade. Place veal in a large roasting pan. Roast the meat for 20 minutes, then add potatoes and garlic. Roast another hour, or until the internal temperature registers 160°F (for well done) on your instant-read meat thermometer. While roast is cooking, bring reserved marinade to a boil in a small saucepan, then cool. Remove roast and let it rest before slicing. Remove potatoes.

Squeeze the roasted cloves of garlic from their skins. Mash and mix with the mayonnaise. Whisk enough of the cooked marinade into the mayonnaise to give it the consistency of a sauce. Serve with the roast and potatoes.

London Broil

Traditionally, the term *London broil* meant a flank steak, grilled and then thinly sliced diagonally across the grain. Now you see the term applied to other cuts of meat, such as round steak, sirloin tip or even chuck. To my mind, these cuts simply do not have the flavor or consistency for a true London broil. This recipe goes well with Lemon Potatoes (see recipe page 116).

☙

Spread the meat flat in a glass baking dish no bigger than necessary to hold the meat. Mix the dressing with the additional lemon juice. Pour dressing over the meat. Marinate, turning several times, for a couple of hours at room temperature, or longer if put in the refrigerator.

Preheat the grill. Remove the meat from the marinade. Season with salt and pepper. Grill over hot coals. The cooking time will depend upon the thickness of the meat, but plan on approximately 5 minutes per side for rare (if meat was at room temperature when cooked).

Slice diagonally into 1/4-inch-thick slices. Serve immediately.

1 flank steak (2 to 2 1/2 pounds)

1 cup Lemon Garlic Dressing (see recipe page 71)

2 tablespoons fresh lemon juice

Salt and freshly ground black pepper to taste

- Serves 6 to 8

Blair's Lemon Pasta

1½ cups all-purpose flour, plus a bit more to flour work surface

1 large egg, at room temperature

1 egg white, at room temperature

1 tablespoon olive oil

1 teaspoon salt

3 tablespoons freshly grated lemon zest

About 2 teaspoons fresh lemon juice

- Makes about ¾ pound

*M*aking homemade pasta is well worth the effort. I'm not saying you will make it every day, but it's great fun to do occasionally with a group of friends. Invite them over to take turns rolling and cutting the pasta. I prefer to mix my dough the old-fashioned way, but you can put all of the ingredients in the bowl of your food processor and process until well blended, adding lemon juice if the mixture is too dry.

I bought my old-fashioned, crank-handled pasta machine in Naples some 27 years ago. Kneading and rolling by hand produces a better consistency of pasta, but it takes a bit of practice. I suggest sticking with your pasta machine unless you decide to become a perfectionist. Nothing makes a home more inviting than pasta hung everywhere to dry. You can buy spaghetti racks to dry your pasta, but why pay that price when you can get a good wooden clothes rack for much less?

This is a very simple pasta recipe. I have given you small amounts to start with, but feel free to double the recipe. You will probably have to make this a couple of times before you get the hang of it and can judge the amount you wish to make. Cut the dough into any shape you desire, and remember that fresh pasta cooks almost instantly.

Put flour in a mound on a work surface, preferably wooden. Make a deep well in the middle of the flour. Beat the egg and egg white lightly with a fork. Pour eggs, olive oil, salt, and lemon zest into the well. Mix together with a fork or your fingers until the dough can be gathered into a rough ball. Put a few drops of lemon juice on the remaining bits of flour on the board and scrape together into the ball of dough. If mixture is too crumbly, add a few drops more lemon juice.

Knead the dough on a floured board for about 10 minutes, working in a bit more flour if the dough is sticky. Dough should be smooth, elastic, and shiny. (You can use a pasta machine to knead the dough, but it is really better to do this by hand.)

Wrap the dough in plastic wrap and let it rest for at least 30 minutes. Cut dough into quarters and roll each section by hand or with your pasta machine until thin. Cut rolled dough into desired shape.

Spread the cut pasta out to dry for 5 to 10 minutes. Cook in boiling salted water until barely tender, just seconds.

Drain well. Serve immediately with preferred sauce.

Cold, Fresh Summer Tomato Sauce

10 ripe plum tomatoes

3 cloves garlic, put through a
garlic press

4 or 5 green onions, thinly sliced

10 or 12 fresh basil leaves,
shredded or chopped

1/3 cup fresh lemon juice

1/3 cup olive oil, or more to taste

1 teaspoon salt, or more to taste

1/4 cup chopped oil-cured black
olives (optional)

Freshly ground black pepper to
taste

- Makes about 2 cups

*T*hat is quite a mouthful for a small recipe. In Italy it would simply be called Pasta Bizanzia, which means cold, fresh tomato sauce served over hot pasta. If you have never had this combination, you are in for a real treat. This versatile sauce can also be used on sandwiches, in salads (bean or other), on cold meats and on vegetables. It may be one of my 10 most favorite recipes, and that's saying something!

You must use the reddest vine-ripened tomatoes you can find, preferably homegrown or from your local veggie stand. I prefer to use plum tomatoes because they are not as juicy, but you certainly can use other varieties.

❧

Bring a saucepan of water to the boil. Drop the tomatoes into boiling water and count slowly to 10. Remove with slotted spoon. Peel tomatoes (the skins will slip off easily). Cut the tomatoes in half and squeeze out the seeds. Chop tomatoes coarsely. Drain well in a nonreactive strainer for 15 minutes. Put the tomatoes in a bowl. Add the remaining ingredients. Stir well. It is good to let the sauce sit for a short period of time at room temperature before serving.

Lemon Pesto

Pesto seems to have a certain cachet these days, and this recipe will make you stand out from the crowd and its ordinary pesto. You can also use this sauce to make a very unusual garlic bread, or spread on focaccia before baking. When you serve this with lemon pasta, you can call it lemon pesto pasta.

⁓

Finely grind the almonds or pine nuts in a blender or small food processor.

Add the lemon zest and garlic. Blend well. Add basil leaves. Leave the motor running and slowly pour oil into the nut mixture until well combined. Add Parmesan cheese and lemon juice. Blend. Check seasoning. Add salt and pepper.

1/4 cup blanched whole almonds or pine nuts

1 tablespoon freshly grated lemon zest

2 large cloves garlic, cut into pieces

3 cups torn fresh basil leaves

1/2 cup fruity olive oil

1/3 cup grated Parmesan cheese, plus additional to serve on top of pasta

1 tablespoon fresh lemon juice

Salt and freshly ground black pepper to taste

- Makes about 1 cup

Risotto al Limone *(Lemon Rice)*

4 tablespoons (1/2 stick) unsalted
butter

1 onion, finely chopped

2 cloves garlic, minced

4 to 5 cups chicken stock

1 1/2 cups Italian arborio rice

3/4 cup fresh lemon juice

Salt and freshly ground black
pepper to taste

1/2 cup grated Parmesan cheese,
preferably imported

- Serves 6 to 8 as a side dish

I love saying *risotto al limone*, or even just *limone*.
It rolls off the tongue so well and reminds me
of eating this dish for the first time in Taro-
mina, Italy, on the coast of Sicily. This recipe calls for
Italian arborio rice, a short-grained rice with a high
starch content. The cooking method of adding the liquid
in small amounts allows the grains of rice to swell to
maximum size and also allows each grain to remain sep-
arate. You can make this with regular rice by replacing
some of the water with fresh lemon juice. Cook as usual.

❧

Heat butter in a heavy 2-quart saucepan. Cook onion
and garlic over medium heat until soft.

Meanwhile, bring chicken stock to a boil and keep
hot on the burner. Add rice to onion mixture and cook,
stirring constantly, until rice grains become opaque and
glisten slightly. Add 1/2 cup of chicken stock to the rice,
stirring, until the liquid is absorbed by the rice. Add 3
cups hot chicken stock in 1/2-cup increments, letting
the rice absorb each addition before adding more. Stir
often. Add lemon juice. Cook until absorbed by the
rice. Check rice for doneness. Add more chicken stock
and cook until rice is tender. All together, rice should
cook 25 to 30 minutes. Stir in salt, pepper, and
Parmesan cheese.

Soubise

This dish is part of my Easter dinner tradition, along with ham and leg of lamb. I am always surprised at how many people are strangers to this tastiest of rice dishes. It is easy to prepare and takes little attention once you put it in the oven. The classic French dish doesn't include lemon, of course, but I find the lemon complements the sweetness of the onions. It is even better the day after. I usually double this recipe to ensure I have some leftovers to give my guests to take home. This recipe is adapted from Julia Child's French Chef series.

❧

Preheat oven to 325°F.

Bring 4 quarts of salted water to a boil. Drop rice into water and boil exactly 5 minutes. Drain well.

Melt butter in a heavy, ovenproof casserole. Stir in the onions and coat well with butter. Stir in the rice, salt, and Lemon Pepper. Cover. Bake, stirring occasionally, until the rice and onions are melded and have become a golden brown, about 1 1/2 to 2 hours. Stir occasionally. Taste for seasoning. Stir in cream and Swiss cheese just before serving.

1/2 cup rice

4 tablespoons (1/2 stick) unsalted butter

7 cups thinly sliced yellow onions

1 teaspoon salt

1 teaspoon Lemon Pepper (see recipe page 24)

1/4 cup heavy cream

1/4 cup grated Swiss cheese

• Serves 6

Vegetables

THERE SEEM TO be a growing number of people today who make vegetables and grains the mainstay of their diets. When alone, I will often make a meal of one or more vegetables, simply prepared—with a squeeze of lemon juice, of course. I don't believe there is a vegetable out there that can't be helped by a little lemon juice, particularly the sweet vegetables such as carrots or squash. To avoid bleaching the color out of green vegetables, add the lemon juice right before serving. White vegetables, on the other hand, will stay nice and white if you add a bit of lemon juice to the cooking water.

My childhood memories are of lots of fresh vegetables in the summer growing season—and nothing but squash, cabbage and canned vegetables in the winter. We should be eternally grateful for today's year-round selection. The microwave has made fixing vegetables fast, but vegetables roasted in the oven have a much more concentrated flavor and remain juicy. Just toss together one vegetable or a medley (always with red peppers for color) with a touch of olive oil, a few squeezes of lemon juice, garlic and herbs and roast about 20 minutes at 400°F. If you are grilling in the summertime, slice vegetables, brush with olive oil, sprinkle with Lemon Pepper and herbs of your choice and cook with your meat. Make extra to serve the next day plain or in a salad. And don't forget pureed vegetables; they are not just for babies. When I lived at Manchester College, Oxford, they served lots of mashed, seasoned veggies that I grew to appreciate well.

We all have our food weaknesses. Mine is potatoes, fixed any way. Thus, you will note several potato recipes in this chapter. Potatoes marry very well with a little lemon.

Stir-fried Lemon Asparagus

2 pounds asparagus

2 tablespoons sesame oil

2 cloves garlic, minced

4 green onions, cut lengthwise
　　into strips

1 can water chestnuts, sliced

1 chicken or vegetarian bouillon
　　cube

3 tablespoons fresh lemon juice

2 teaspoons grated lemon zest

2 to 3 teaspoons soy sauce

Salt and freshly ground black
　　pepper to taste

● Serves 6

*E*very spring, lovely little asparagus heads poke
through the soil. And every spring while growing
up, my brother and I would rise at the crack of
dawn and go to Mrs. Weiss's asparagus patch and pick
asparagus. Or should I say cut asparagus, since we used a
V-shaped cutting tool not unlike a long-handled weed
digger. Unless you have your own asparagus patch, you
may never experience the unbelievable flavor of freshly
picked asparagus. In fact, it is not difficult to grow—if
you put the plants in properly. I say that because, even
with stellar knowledge of this vegetable, I once put in a
bed of asparagus pointing the roots up.

This is a Chinese-inspired dish. Stir-frying is quick and
easy, even if you don't have a wok. This will go well with
grilled meats. Personally, I don't like asparagus with fish.

ॐ

Wash and dry asparagus and break off the tough part of
the stems. Cut diagonally into 2-inch pieces. Heat oil
in a nonstick frying pan or wok over medium-high
heat. Stir-fry garlic for 1 minute. Add green onions.
Stir-fry for 1 minute. Add asparagus and water chestnuts. Stir-fry for about 3 minutes. Add bouillon cube,
lemon juice, lemon zest, and soy sauce. Cook another
minute or so, until asparagus is crisp-tender and all
ingredients are heated through. Taste for seasoning.
Serve immediately.

Green Beans with Garlic and Lemon

I can never decide whether to call this dish garlic and green beans or green beans and garlic. Either way, this is a lot of garlic. It is hard to measure anyone's tolerance level for garlic, but people love this dish. Do not attempt to measure the garlic. This is not really a recipe, but more of a suggested procedure. Whatever you do, don't overcook the beans. They should be crisp-tender, not wet noodles.

ℬℯ

Cook green beans in a large pot of boiling, salted water until barely tender. Drain well. Toss with butter. Add minced garlic, lemon zest, salt, and Lemon Pepper to taste. Toss well. Serve immediately.

1 pound green beans, trimmed of tails

2 tablespoons unsalted butter

About 2 tablespoons minced garlic (this is the minimum; add more to taste)

1 teaspoon freshly grated lemon zest

Salt and Lemon Pepper (see recipe page 24) to taste

- Serves 6

Shredded Carrot Sauté

2 tablespoons unsalted butter or
olive oil

1 pound carrots, peeled and
coarsely shredded

5 or 6 green onions, thinly sliced

Salt and freshly ground black
pepper to taste

Juice from 1 lemon

Serves 8

*C*arrots have a natural sweetness that pairs so well with the tart lemon. A few squeezes of lemon juice over any carrot recipe will create a most interesting taste. I would venture to bet that after trying it you'll never serve carrots without lemon again. The following recipe is one of my favorites because it is so simple, so fast and a terrific, eye-appealing vegetable on the dinner plate. You can sprinkle the carrots with an herb of your choice. I like dill for a change of pace. You can also add a bit of grated ginger while cooking. Any leftovers are good cold as a salad.

ॐ

Melt butter or oil in a large nonstick frying pan. Sauté carrots and green onions over medium heat until carrots are crisp-tender. Stir in salt and pepper to taste. Add lemon juice, stirring well to blend the flavors. Serve warm.

Lemon Chive Brussels Sprouts

When buying Brussels sprouts, try to pick ones of a uniform size with no brown on the leaves. If you cut X's on the core ends of the sprouts, it will hasten cooking.

❦

Cook Brussels sprouts in boiling water until crisp-tender. Drain.

Melt butter in saucepan. Add cooked Brussels sprouts and remaining ingredients. Cook, stirring, until heated through.

1 pound Brussels sprouts, washed and trimmed

2 tablespoons unsalted butter

2 tablespoons snipped fresh chives

3 tablespoons freshly grated lemon zest

2 teaspoons snipped fresh dill

Salt and freshly ground black pepper to taste

- Serves 4

Best Beets Ever

1 pound fresh beets

2 tablespoons unsalted butter

5 or 6 green onions, thinly sliced

Salt and Lemon Pepper (see recipe page 24) to taste

1/4 cup fresh lemon juice

- Serves 4

*G*orgeous red beets can dress up any plate. Most unfortunately, many people associate beets with an overcooked vegetable or with the pickled beets on the salad bar at a buffet restaurant. In fact, cooked properly, beets are very tasty. When I am lucky enough to find a bunch of small beets, I will roast them until tender, peel and slice, then toss with a bit of butter and lemon juice. The recipe I give you here is faster, but equally good. When cooking beets, always remember to keep whole, with about an inch of the green left, and not to break the skin, or the red color will bleed.

ৡৱ

Cut tops off beets. Do not cut root ends. Put beets in a medium saucepan. Cover and bring to a boil. Reduce heat and simmer for about 10 minutes to partially cook beets. Larger beets will take longer. Remove from water. Cool. Carefully peel and slice.

Melt butter in frying pan. Sauté green onions over medium heat for a minute. Add sliced beets. Cook, stirring occasionally, until beets are tender, about 10 to 15 minutes. Season with salt and pepper to taste. Add lemon juice. Stir well. Serve warm.

Stir-fried Fennel and Garlic

Europeans make such good use of fennel, or *finocchio*, as the Italians call it. Fennel is good blanched for salads or cooked as a vegetable dish. The licorice flavor diminishes when fennel is cooked. Chewing on raw fennel is reputed to help curb your appetite. I can't attest to that.

Heat olive oil in a nonstick frying pan or wok. Stir-fry the onion and garlic for a minute over medium-high heat. Add the fennel and lemon zest. Stir-fry until fennel begins to brown and is crisp-tender, about 10 to 15 minutes. Season with salt and pepper. Add lemon juice. Stir well. Serve immediately.

2 tablespoons olive oil

1 onion, thinly sliced

2 cloves garlic, minced

4 fennel bulbs, ends and coarse outer layer trimmed, sliced

1 tablespoon grated lemon zest

Salt and freshly ground black pepper to taste

2 tablespoons fresh lemon juice

- Serves 4

Lemon Potatoes

1 pound small, red new potatoes, cut in half, or large potatoes, quartered

4 cloves garlic, chopped

2 large onions, cut in eighths

3 tablespoons olive oil

2 tablespoons fresh lemon juice

1 teaspoon salt

1 teaspoon Lemon Pepper (see recipe page 24)

- Serves 4

I adore potatoes prepared in any way. I once went on a potato diet and lost eight pounds in a week. I had potatoes all day in many forms; I never felt hungry, never had that diet headache and had lots of energy. I often have a potato before going to the gym to work out. Potatoes are full of vitamins and minerals and are not fattening. A little lemon and you won't miss the butter or sour cream. Keep in mind: Potatoes love lemons.

გა

Preheat oven to 400°F.

Toss together all ingredients. Spray a shallow-sided baking pan with no-stick cooking spray or line with aluminum foil. Spread potato mixture in pan. Allow enough room so the potatoes do not touch and can brown well.

Bake in the oven, stirring once or twice, until potatoes are tender and nicely browned. This should take about 25 to 30 minutes.

Baked Potato Wedges

If you love the thick and tasty potato wedges often served in restaurants with soups or sandwiches, you will greatly appreciate this recipe. It's just as good, but with almost no fat and certainly fewer calories. Try the recipe first as is, then branch out with your own favorite seasonings, such as chili powder or one of the dill mixtures on the market.

೮ಎ

Cut the potatoes lengthwise into wedges. Put in a large bowl and toss with olive oil and lemon juice. Let stand for about 45 minutes.

Preheat oven to 400°F.

Toss potatoes with garlic salt, paprika, and Lemon Pepper. Spray a shallow-sided baking pan with no-stick spray or line with aluminum foil. Arrange wedges in single layer in pan. Bake 20 minutes, turning the wedges once and sprinkling with more garlic salt, paprika, and Lemon Pepper. Bake 15 to 20 minutes more, until nicely browned and tender. Check seasoning and add more salt and Lemon Pepper if necessary.

4 large baking potatoes, about 2 pounds, scrubbed and unpeeled

1/3 cup olive oil

1/4 cup fresh lemon juice

2 teaspoons or more garlic salt

Paprika to taste

Lemon Pepper (see recipe page 24) to taste

- Serves 6 to 8

Baked Leeks and Potatoes

4 large leeks, white part only, cleaned and sliced

2 cups chicken or vegetable broth

5 cloves garlic, finely minced

3 pounds boiling potatoes, peeled and sliced

Salt and Lemon Pepper (see recipe page 24) to taste

4 teaspoons fresh rosemary leaves or 2 teaspoons dried rosemary

4 teaspoons fresh lemon thyme leaves or 2 teaspoons dried thyme

1/2 teaspoon dried savory, crumbled

1/2 cup fresh lemon juice

• Serves 8

*T*his is somewhat time-consuming, but your efforts will be rewarded with a homey, fulfilling dish that can be either a side dish or main course with a green vegetable or salad. Please note that there is not one gram of fat added to this dish. There may be a small amount from the chicken broth, but if that bothers you, buy defatted chicken broth.

ℒℐ

Preheat oven to 425°F.

Combine leeks, broth, and garlic in saucepan. Bring to a boil and simmer 5 minutes. Strain the mixture, reserving liquid. Coat a baking dish with no-stick cooking spray. Arrange about a third of the sliced potatoes in the baking dish. Sprinkle liberally with salt and Lemon Pepper. Combine herbs in a small bowl. Sprinkle half over potatoes. Spread half of leek mixture on top of potatoes. Make another layer with half of remaining potatoes, salt, Lemon Pepper, herbs, and leeks, ending with potatoes on top. Combine lemon juice and reserved cooking liquid and pour over the top. Cover with lid or foil. Bake for 30 minutes covered. Uncover and bake for 45 minutes more, or until top is lightly brown. Serve at room temperature.

Roasted Sweet Potatoes with Lemon Butter

The sweet potato cries out for lemon, not marshmallows! Granted, those candied sweet potatoes at Thanksgiving are great, and I certainly ate my share in days past, but now my preference is for a simple sweet potato, baked in the oven and topped with butter and lemon. You can cook these sweet potatoes in the microwave if you are in a hurry, but the flavor will not be as good. P.S. You can get by with a soupçon of butter.

ও

Preheat oven to 400°F.

Cut sweet potatoes in half lengthwise. Prick skins with a fork. Place cut sides down, on a greased baking sheet. Bake until tender, about 30 minutes. Melt butter. Stir in lemon juice, salt, and pepper. Serve lemon butter with sweet potatoes.

4 sweet potatoes or yams, scrubbed and patted dry

4 tablespoons (1/2 stick) unsalted butter

3 to 4 tablespoons fresh lemon juice

1/2 teaspoon salt

Freshly ground black pepper to taste

- Serves 4

Spaghetti Squash Sauté

1 spaghetti squash, about 2 pounds

2 tablespoons olive oil

6 green onions, sliced

2 or 3 cloves garlic, crushed

1 tablespoon finely chopped fresh basil (lemon basil if you have it)

2 tablespoons chopped fresh parsley

Salt to taste

Lemon Pepper (see recipe page 24) to taste

2 to 3 tablespoons fresh lemon juice, or more to taste

• Serves 6

I fought the whole idea of spaghetti squash for the longest time. What a silly name, and how could the inside of a squash possibly resemble spaghetti? Well, it does and I love it. Let me qualify that: I love it fixed any way except with tomato sauce. Cook a couple while you are at it, shred the inside of the extra one and keep in the refrigerator to sauté for another day. Spaghetti squash is also very good baked with garlic, onions, bell peppers and herbs. You can cook the squash in the microwave if you are in a hurry.

৯৯

Preheat oven to 350°F.

Prick the squash with a fork. Bake on rack inside a roasting pan for about an hour, turning once. Cool until you can handle squash comfortably. Cut in half. Scoop out the seeds. Scrape out the flesh with a fork. It will come out looking like spaghetti.

Sauté green onions and garlic in olive oil over medium heat until soft. Stir in the spaghetti squash, basil, parsley, salt, and Lemon Pepper. Cook until heated through. Add lemon juice. Check for seasoning. Serve warm.

Spinach with Caramelized Onions

One of my oldest and dearest friends from South Dakota, Jane Dahl Low, gave me this recipe. She now lives in Moraga, California, and one of the great treats of my life is to visit her and spend days prowling around Berkeley, California, going to all the wonderful bakeries and farm markets. I always return to the East Coast with a suitcase full of produce. Jane says she got this recipe out of a food magazine but doesn't remember which one, so there is no way I can give credit. I have adjusted it a bit to suit my taste. This is a terribly chic dish.

1 large red onion, thinly sliced

2 tablespoons olive oil

1 pound fresh spinach, washed thoroughly, dried, and stems removed

Salt and freshly ground black pepper to taste

4 teaspoons fresh lemon juice

• Serves 4

♚

In a heavy skillet sauté red onion in olive oil over medium-high heat. Stir constantly. The onion will begin to caramelize in about 15 minutes. Continue to cook until part of the onion is dark and crisp, maybe 2 to 3 minutes more.

Immediately add the spinach and cook, stirring, until it is wilted. Remove from heat and season with salt, pepper, and lemon juice. Serve immediately.

Simple Lemon Mushrooms

1 tablespoon unsalted butter

1 tablespoon olive oil

4 cloves garlic, crushed

5 or 6 green onions, sliced

2 pounds small mushrooms, or large mushrooms cut into chunks

1 teaspoon dried tarragon, crumbled

1/2 cup coarsely chopped flat-leaf parsley

1/2 cup fresh lemon juice

Salt and Lemon Pepper (see recipe page 24) to taste

- Serves 8

These mushrooms are so easy to make, and simply divine. I munch so many of these while cooking that I usually make double so that some reach the table. This dish can stand alone as a vegetable, as an addition to pasta or a salad, or as an accompaniment to an entree. It's low in calories and proportionally low in fat. Make good use of the mushroom variety available in the supermarket. Some are a bit pricey, but it takes only a few shitake or portobellos to add flavor.

For a faster version, sauté the mushrooms and sprinkle with garlic salt, Lemon Pepper and onion powder. Squeeze some lemon juice over them just before serving.

❧

Combine butter and oil in a heavy frying pan. Sauté garlic and green onions for a minute or so over medium heat. Raise heat to medium-high and add mushrooms. Cook, stirring occasionally, for 5 to 10 minutes, until mushrooms are tender and beginning to brown. Add tarragon and parsley. Cook for another minute or so. Add lemon juice and salt and pepper to taste. Serve warm.

Desserts

THERE IS A WON-
derful little book titled
Life Is Uncertain . . .
Eat Dessert First! by
Sol Gordon and Harold Brecher. The
authors give some wise advice on finding
joy in life, none of which is better than
the idea suggested by that title. Try
having dessert first for a change. Who
knows how your life might change?

A little dessert never
hurt any normally
healthy person. I grew
up having it at both
dinner and supper. Desserts were fruit—
fresh or canned—puddings, cake or pie.
Cookies were usually for coffee time,
which seemed to happen about 10 times
a day. Every woman had her specialty,
and at all the social functions—church,

school, clubs—the lineup of baked goods was eye-popping.

The interesting part of all this was that, with few exceptions, no one was really fat and no one seemed to diet. I can only specu-late that it was because most people had an active life. Work was hard and there was no television. Now everyone seems to be on a diet of some kind, but that doesn't mean that people don't partake.

You must always remember that *desserts get the most applause*, even from people on a diet, and if you are to become a famous cook, you must have at least one basic and one exotic dessert in your repeat file. I have made a serious effort to include some very easy recipes which are terrif-ic. You'll have no excuse not to shine!

When a recipe here calls for sugar, try using Lemon Gran-ulated Sugar or Lemon Powdered Sugar (see recipes page 33) if possible. When a recipe calls for oil, use Lemon Oil (see recipe page 22) if you have any on hand.

Lemon Carrot Cake

2 cups coarsely shredded carrots

1½ cups finely grated carrots

½ cup seedless raisins

About 1 tablespoon lemon brandy (see page 12) or Lemoncello for macerating raisins

Zest of 3 lemons, removed with potato peeler

1 cup granulated sugar

1 cup brown sugar

8 tablespoons (1 stick) unsalted butter

½ cup vegetable oil

4 large eggs

1 teaspoon fresh lemon juice

1 teaspoon vanilla extract

2 cups plus 1 tablespoon all-purpose, presifted flour, aerated

2 teaspoons baking powder

1 teaspoon baking soda

1 teaspoon salt

2 teaspoons ground cinnamon

½ teaspoon ground mace

This is my adaptation of my mother's old recipe, which she made in a loaf pan. I use a loose-bottom tube pan. I hope you will indulge me in my little idiosyncrasy of grating half of the carrots using the fine holes of the grater to allow them to disappear into the batter and shredding the other half using the coarse holes to provide lovely orange flecks in the cake. This all came about after someone said to me, "There aren't really carrots in this cake, are there?" This cake can do with a little age, say, a couple of days in the refrigerator after frosting.

❦

Preheat oven to 350°F.

Shred carrots; set aside. Put raisins and liquor in dish to macerate.

Process lemon zest with sugars in a food processor. Add butter and oil. Process until smooth. With machine running, add eggs one at a time. Add lemon juice and vanilla. Process until smooth.

In a large bowl, stir together flour, baking powder, baking soda, salt, and spices. Add mixture from processor, stirring well. Add carrots, raisins, and walnuts. Stir to evenly distribute throughout the dough.

Pour into a greased and floured tube pan and bake about 50 minutes. Check with cake tester or toothpick. Cool in pan a few minutes. Remove from pan and frost when completely cool. If using glaze instead of frosting, cake should be warm.

Lemon Cream Cheese Frosting

Carrot and spice cakes cry out for this frosting. Just a bit of lemon cuts the overt sweetness of the sugar. If you want a more pronounced lemon flavor, add more grated lemon zest. For an interesting taste, substitute a tablespoon of lemon brandy or Lemoncello for the lemon juice.

Cream butter and cream cheese. Add remaining ingredients. Beat until smooth.

Lemon Glaze

Use this glaze when you don't want a thick icing.

Combine all ingredients in a large mixing bowl. Beat until smooth. Mixture will be thin. Pour glaze over warm cake. Some glaze will end up on your cake plate; spoon it back over until cake is nicely covered.

$1/4$ teaspoon ground nutmeg

$1/4$ teaspoon ground cloves

1 cup walnuts, coarsely chopped

CREAM CHEESE FROSTING

6 tablespoons ($3/4$ stick) unsalted butter or margarine

4 ounces cream cheese, at room temperature

1 teaspoon finely grated lemon zest

2 teaspoons fresh lemon juice

Pinch of salt

2 cups confectioners' sugar

LEMON GLAZE

4 tablespoons ($1/2$ stick) unsalted butter, softened

2 cups confectioners' sugar

$1/3$ cup lemon juice

Pinch of salt

1 tablespoon finely grated lemon zest

• Serves 10 to 12

127

Lemon Chocolate Cake

4 large eggs

2 cups granulated sugar

1/2 cup light brown sugar

8 tablespoons (1 stick) unsalted butter

2 teaspoons vanilla extract

1 1/2 cups all-purpose, presifted flour

1/2 teaspoon salt

2/3 cup cocoa powder

1 tablespoon baking powder

1/4 cup fresh lemon juice

1/4 cup fresh orange juice

1 1/4 cups pecans, chopped

Confectioners' sugar or Lemon Powdered Sugar (see recipe page 33)

- Serves 8 to 10

*T*his is the best of all worlds, combining the light, refreshing lemon with dark, dense, satisfying chocolate. This cake is good by itself with a dusting of Lemon Powdered Sugar, but sublime when paired with ice cream or lemon whipped cream. It will fall a bit when removed from the oven, but not to worry. I think it's about impossible to harm this cake.

૪ꝋ

Preheat oven to 350°F.

Beat eggs, sugars, butter, and vanilla until lemon-colored. Stir together flour, salt, cocoa powder, and baking powder. Blend flour mixture, lemon juice, orange juice, and pecans into egg mixture.

Pour into a greased and floured tube or bundt pan. Bake for about 35 to 40 minutes, or until cake begins to pull away from the sides of the pan and is springy to the touch. Cool. Remove from pan and dust with confectioners' sugar or Lemon Powdered Sugar.

Pain de Gênes (French Almond Cake)

This is one of my signature dishes. It always appears on my Easter buffet table. I have been making this cake since I was a young bride and first learned to grind almonds. The lemon addition came later. Pain de Gênes is a small, single-layer, dense cake. It is perfect to serve with some fresh fruit or chocolate mousse. Grind the almonds in a small spice grinder. Food processors do not do a good job. I grind a lot at once and freeze what I don't use. You'll be amazed at the recipes that benefit from a bit of ground almond.

※

Preheat oven to 350°F.

Butter an 8-inch cake pan with removable bottom or 8-inch springform pan. Cut a piece of wax paper to fit the bottom. Butter wax paper.

Cream butter and sugar. Add ground almonds and beat for 1 minute. Beat in eggs, one at a time, for 1½ minutes after each addition. Beat in lemon zest, baking powder, almond extract, and liquor. Combine flour and salt. Carefully fold into creamed mixture a tablespoon at a time.

Bake 40 to 45 minutes, until cake is golden brown and you can see a little line of shrinkage around the edge. Unmold onto a rack. Cool. Sprinkle with confectioners' sugar.

8 tablespoons (1 stick) unsalted butter, slightly softened

3/4 cup granulated sugar

3/4 cup ground blanched almonds

3 large eggs

2 tablespoons finely grated fresh lemon zest

1/8 teaspoon baking powder

1/2 teaspoon almond extract

1 tablespoon Lemoncello, lemon brandy (see page 12), rum, or kirsch

1/2 cup sifted cake flour

Pinch of salt

Confectioners' sugar

• Serves 8

129

Fluffy Lemon Pudding Cake

2 eggs, separated

1 cup granulated sugar

1 cup milk

3 tablespoons all-purpose flour

Grated zest of 1 lemon

Juice of 1 lemon

1/2 teaspoon salt

- Serves 6

In England, dessert is often referred to as the pudding or "pudd." (Kind of fun to say "Are you ready for your pudd?") No doubt the term goes back centuries as well may this pudding cake. It is certainly old-fashioned and has numerous versions. All are characterized by the magic separation of the ingredients into two distinct layers as it bakes—a creamy base topped by a sponge cake top. No whipped cream is necessary.

This pudd is easy to make. It is baked in a pan of water, which sounds like a big deal but isn't at all.

❧

Preheat oven to 325°F.

In a large bowl, beat egg yolks with 3/4 cup sugar until lemon-yellow. Add milk, flour, lemon zest, lemon juice, and salt. Beat to mix well.

In a medium bowl with clean beaters, beat egg whites until stiff. Add remaining 1/4 cup sugar and beat until stiff but not dry. Fold beaten egg whites into lemon mixture.

Turn mixture into a buttered 1 1/2-quart casserole and place in a baking pan. Pour enough hot water into baking pan to come 3/4 of the way up the sides of the casserole. Bake 50 to 60 minutes, or until a knife inserted in center comes out clean. Leaving the pan of water in the oven, carefully remove the casserole. Serve at room temperature.

Lemon Pound Cake

Classic pound cake is made with one pound each of butter, sugar, flour and eggs. The proportions have changed with the times, but a good pound cake is still rich and moist. My recipe breaks some pound cake rules by throwing all the ingredients in a bowl and mixing, but the results are good enough for me. This cake is so good with fresh fruit. You can also toast a piece for a very, very special breakfast treat. This cake ages and freezes very well, so make two while you're at it.

୫ঌ

Preheat oven to 325°F.

Combine all cake ingredients in a large bowl. Beat at high speed for 4 to 5 minutes. Pour into a greased and floured tube pan.

Bake for 55 to 60 minutes, or until a cake tester or toothpick comes out clean. Cool in pan for 10 to 15 minutes.

Meanwhile, make glaze. Blend lemon juice and confectioners' sugar well until sugar is dissolved. Remove cake from pan. Poke the cake several times with a toothpick. Cool slightly. Pour glaze over the warm (not hot) cake. Cool before serving.

1 cup (2 sticks) unsalted butter, softened

2 cups granulated sugar

2 tablespoons fresh lemon juice

1 cup buttermilk

4 eggs

3 cups all-purpose, presifted flour, aerated a bit

1 teaspoon salt

1/2 teaspoon baking soda

1/2 teaspoon baking powder

1/2 teaspoon vanilla extract

3 tablespoons finely grated lemon zest

GLAZE

1/2 cup fresh lemon juice

1/2 cup confectioners' sugar

- Serves 12

Tiny Lemon Tarts

PASTRY SHELLS

8 tablespoons (1 stick) unsalted butter or margarine, slightly softened

A 3-ounce package cream cheese, at room temperature

1 cup all-purpose flour

1/8 teaspoon salt

1 tablespoon finely grated fresh lemon zest

Solid shortening for greasing muffin tins

LEMON FILLING

1/3 cup fresh lemon juice

2 tablespoons finely grated lemon zest

1/2 cup granulated sugar

2 large eggs, beaten

4 tablespoons (1/2 stick) unsalted butter

● Makes 2 dozen

I hope you love these cute little lemon morsels as much as I do. *They are easy.* They are so perfect to serve at a buffet when you want a dessert that is finger-friendly and can be passed on a platter. If you don't happen to have little muffin pans, run get some. Ideally you should serve these the day they're made.

৪৯

To make the pastry shells, cream butter with cream cheese until smooth. Add the flour, salt, and lemon zest. Mix well. Chill dough for 1 hour.

Preheat oven to 425°F. Grease muffin tins with shortening. Divide dough into 24 balls. This is easier if you use a melon scoop. Press dough onto bottom and sides of muffin tins, forming pastry cups. Bake for about 8 minutes, or until pastry is light golden brown. Cool completely before filling.

Combine all filling ingredients in top of double boiler over boiling water. Cook, stirring constantly, until mixture thickens, about 15 minutes. The mixture will thicken more after cooling. Cool thoroughly. Pour into baked shells. Just before serving, top with fresh fruit.

Warm Plum Torte

When prune plums come into season at the end of the summer, I make one of these tortes every week. I also freeze a couple to pull out in the middle of winter. I like serving this plain, without a topping, to let the tart plum taste mingle with the rich cake, but you could plunk a spoonful of whipped cream or lemon sauce on top. I think I risk little if I tell you this is foolproof.

❦

Preheat oven to 350°F.

Cream sugar and butter. Add flour, baking powder, salt, eggs, and lemon zest. Beat well. Spoon batter into a greased and floured 8-inch springform pan or pie plate. Place plum halves on top, skin side up or down, as you prefer. Pour lemon juice over all. Sprinkle with sugar and cinnamon.

Bake 50 to 60 minutes, or until cake is nicely brown and shrinks slightly from pan. Remove from the oven. Cool. Remove from pan. Serve slightly warm.

3/4 cup granulated sugar

8 tablespoons (1 stick) unsalted butter or margarine

1 cup all-purpose flour, sifted

1 teaspoon baking powder

1 teaspoon salt

2 large eggs

1 tablespoon freshly grated lemon zest

12 to 16 prune plums (small size is better), halved and pitted

2 tablespoons fresh lemon juice

Granulated sugar

Cinnamon

- Serves 6 to 8

Shredded Apple Tart

Lemon Pie Crust (see recipes page 135), made in a 10-inch tart pan

4 to 6 tablespoons apricot jam

3 large or 4 medium-sized, tart cooking apples

1/3 cup fresh lemon juice

4 egg yolks

1/2 cup granulated sugar (preferably Lemon Granulated Sugar; see recipe page 33)

1/2 cup finely ground almonds

1/3 cup golden raisins

1/2 teaspoon ground cinnamon

2 tablespoons melted unsalted butter

• Serves 8 to 10

*L*iving as I do in the heart of the Winchester, Virginia, apple country, I can hardly wait for the new crop to be picked each fall. The hills for miles around are full of apple trees of many varieties. This recipe is my adaptation of the late Simone Beck's recipe. I have replaced some of the butter in the original recipe with lemon juice.

ঞ

If using the Press-in-Pan Pie Crust, prebake as instructed on page 135. Preheat oven to 350°F.

Spread the apricot jam on the bottom of the pie crust.

Peel apples and toss with lemon juice. Coarsely grate or shred them onto a kitchen towel. Reserve leftover lemon juice; you should have at least 1/4 cup. Bring up sides of towel around apples and squeeze to remove moisture. Beat egg yolks. Add sugar and beat until thick and lemon-colored.

Add ground almonds and raisins. Stir. Add apples and cinnamon. Stir well. Pour mixture into pastry shell. Bake for 20 minutes. Remove from oven. Prick top of tart in several places. Pour 1/4 cup of reserved lemon juice over tart. Pour melted butter over the tart.

Return to oven. Bake 20 minutes more. Serve warm with ice cream or whipped cream.

Lemon Pie Crust

Lemon does a great job livening up pastry, particularly pie crust. Both of these recipes can be wrapped in plastic and stored in the freezer for a couple of months.

Rolling-Pin Pie Crust

Mix flour and salt. Cut in butter, shortening, and lemon peel with a pastry blender. Add enough lemon juice to make a dough soft enough to form into a ball. Wrap in plastic and refrigerate for at least an hour before rolling.

Press-in-Pan Pie Crust

Pulse the flour, sugar, salt, lemon zest, and butter in food processor until mixture looks like cornmeal. Mix lemon juice and vanilla. Pulse into flour mixture until it forms a ball. Wrap in plastic wrap and refrigerate for 30 minutes.

Press into pie plate or tart pan and freeze for 30 minutes before prebaking. Prebake at 425°F for at least 10 minutes.

ROLLING-PIN PIE CRUST

- 1 1/4 cups all-purpose, presifted flour

- 1/2 teaspoon salt

- 4 tablespoons (1/2 stick) unsalted butter, cut into pieces

- 1/4 cup solid shortening

- 1 tablespoon finely grated fresh lemon zest

- 2 to 3 tablespoons fresh lemon juice

- Makes enough for one 9-inch pie or one 10-inch tart

PRESS-IN-PAN PIE CRUST

- 1 cup all-purpose, presifted flour

- 1 tablespoon granulated sugar

- 1/2 teaspoon salt

- 2 tablespoons finely grated fresh lemon zest

- 8 tablespoons (1 stick) unsalted butter

- 1 tablespoon fresh lemon juice

- 1/2 teaspoon vanilla extract

- Makes enough for one 9-inch pie or one 10-inch tart

Really Lemony Bars

CRUST

1 cup all-purpose, presifted flour

¼ cup confectioners' sugar

8 tablespoons (1 stick) unsalted butter

1 tablespoon finely grated fresh lemon zest

Solid shortening for greasing pan

LEMON FILLING

2 large eggs

1 cup granulated sugar

½ cup fresh lemon juice

2 tablespoons finely grated fresh lemon zest

2 tablespoons all-purpose flour

Pinch of salt

Confectioners' sugar

- Makes 16 squares

*L*emon bars seem to have been around forever. I always make them when I have foreign visitors. And they almost always ask for the recipe. This is the one my mother gave me years ago, except that I put in a lot more lemon juice. They are tart indeed. This recipe makes enough for an 8-inch pan. Small, you say? Well yes, but if I made more, I'd eat more.

ℒ

Preheat oven to 325°F.

To make the crust, combine all crust ingredients in a food processor and process until mixture resembles coarse crumbs, or combine with a pastry cutter by hand. Lightly grease an 8-inch square pan with shortening. Press mixture into pan.

Bake in middle of oven for 20 minutes, until slightly golden in color. Remove from oven. Raise oven temperature to 350°F.

To make the filling, beat eggs until light and fluffy. Add sugar and beat until thick and lemon-colored. Beat in lemon juice, grated lemon zest, flour, and salt. Pour into prepared crust.

Bake in upper third of oven until filling is set, about 20 minutes. Cool. Dust with confectioners' sugar. Cut into bars.

Easy Refrigerator Lemon Cookies

This is one of my favorite lemon cookie recipes. These are simplicity itself to make, but you will need to allow for the dough to firm a couple of hours in the refrigerator before baking, so plan ahead. I have been known to snitch pieces and pieces of this dough. You really have to like something to keep opening the refrigerator and unwrapping and wrapping cookie dough. These cookies are particularly nice in the summertime, with a bowl of fresh fruit salad.

Zest from 1 large lemon

1 cup granulated sugar

1 cup (2 sticks) unsalted butter, chilled and cut into pieces

2 1/3 cups cake flour, sifted

1/2 teaspoon baking soda

1/2 teaspoon salt

- Makes about 5 dozen

Process the lemon zest and sugar in a food processor until the zest is as fine as the sugar. Add the butter. Process until fluffy. Scrape down the bowl. Add the flour, baking soda, and salt. Process briefly until mixed. Form dough into two 1 1/2-inch-round logs and wrap each in wax paper. Refrigerate until firm.

Preheat oven to 350°F.

Slice each log into 1/4-inch-thick cookies and place on an ungreased baking sheet. Bake for 8 to 10 minutes, until golden around the edges. Do not overbake.

Lemon Mousse

1 envelope unflavored gelatin

1/3 cup cold water

4 eggs, separated

1/2 cup fresh lemon juice

1/4 teaspoon salt

1 cup granulated sugar

1/8 teaspoon cinnamon

1/8 teaspoon nutmeg

1/2 teaspoon almond extract

1 tablespoon Grand Marnier
liqueur (optional)

1 cup heavy cream

1/4 cup confectioners' sugar

• Serves 6

ousse is another one of those words I love to say. It sounds so elegant, which it is, and so elaborate, which it isn't. This is such a lovely, refreshing dessert, particularly after a heavy meal. I like to garnish it with some Candied Lemon Peel and serve with a chocolate truffle or a piece of fresh fruit. You can put Lemon Mousse in a single dish or in champagne glasses, or you can fill a prepared crumb crust and serve it as a pie.

❧

Soften gelatin in cold water. Combine egg yolks, lemon juice, salt, 1/2 cup of the sugar, cinnamon, and nutmeg in the top of a double boiler. Cook over boiling water, stirring constantly, until slightly thickened. Do not boil. Add gelatin mixture and almond extract. Stir well. Remove from heat. Cool. Stir in Grand Marnier.

Beat egg whites until foamy. Gradually add remaining 1/2 cup of sugar to egg whites and beat until stiff peaks form. Whip cream with confectioners' sugar. Fold egg whites and cream into cooled gelatin mixture and pour into a pretty dish. Refrigerate for at least 3 hours before serving. Garnish with Candied Lemon Peel or Candied Lemon Threads.

Candied Lemon Peel

I like to make this around Christmas time to give as gifts. You can also make this recipe with orange peel.

Cut the lemon zest into uniform sizes. Combine 6 cups cold water and lemon zest in a saucepan. Bring to a boil and boil for 10 minutes. Drain and rinse zest. Repeat the process with 6 additional cups water. Drain.

Combine remaining ingredients in a heavy saucepan and bring to a boil. Boil for 1 minute. Add drained zest and simmer for 45 minutes, stirring occasionally. Zest will be transparent.

Remove zest and toss with 1/2 cup sugar to coat. Spread out to dry on tray. Store in a tightly covered container.

Candied Lemon Threads

This preparation is simpler and faster than the Candied Lemon Peel.

Place all ingredients in a small, heavy saucepan. Cook until sugar is completely dissolved. Simmer, stirring occasionally, until the lemon zest has absorbed most of the syrup, 10 to 15 minutes. Cool. Remove lemon threads. Spread out to dry on tray.

CANDIED LEMON PEEL

3 cups lemon zest in strips

12 cups cold water

2 cups granulated sugar

1 1/2 cups boiling water

1 tablespoon Grand Marnier

1 whole allspice

A 1-inch piece of vanilla bean

About 1/2 cup granulated sugar to coat cooked zest

CANDIED LEMON THREADS

1/2 cup water

Zest from 3 lemons, using a lemon zester

1/3 cup plus 1 tablespoon granulated sugar

Strawberry-Rhubarb Sherbet

4 cups small rhubarb pieces

1/2 cup water

2 cups granulated sugar

2 or 3 strips lemon zest

1 pint fresh strawberries, washed and hulled

1/4 cup fresh lemon juice

1/8 teaspoon salt

3/4 cup heavy cream

- Serves 6

Some food combinations are made in heaven, and strawberries and rhubarb is one of them. Almost everyone I knew growing up had rhubarb plants in their yard.

I have two sizes of the Donvier-type ice cream maker, the cylinders of which I keep in my freezer all summer to make fresh fruit ices and ice cream. I find these to be the easiest for me, but use whatever type of ice cream maker suits you.

૪ͻ

Cook rhubarb, water, sugar, and lemon zest in a nonreactive saucepan until soft, about 5 to 10 minutes. Cool.

Puree strawberries in a food processor or blender. Press strawberries and cooked rhubarb through a sieve. Add remaining ingredients, mixing well. Process in an ice cream maker according to manufacturer's instructions.

Lemon Cream Cheese Pie with Blueberries

Some desserts seem to cycle in popularity. A few years ago, this dish was very popular made with cream cheese, condensed milk and a can of cherry pie filling on top. Pretty rich. This is a down-sized version, if you will. There is now a nonfat, sweetened condensed milk on the market that is simply wonderful. You can use it to replace the full-fat version in all your recipes. You can still top the pie with a can of pie filling, but it is ever so much nicer if you puree some fresh fruit, swirl it throughout the batter and serve with fresh fruit on top.

Beat the cream cheese until fluffy. Continue to beat as you slowly pour the condensed milk into the cream cheese. Beat until smooth. Stir in lemon juice, lemon zest, and vanilla. Pour into prepared crust.

Puree 1/3 cup blueberries or other fruit. Drizzle on top of prepared pie. Run a knife through the pie to create a swirled effect. Refrigerate for 3 to 4 hours. Top with remaining blueberries or other fruit.

An 8-ounce package cream cheese, at room temperature

A 14-ounce can sweetened condensed milk, regular, low-fat, or nonfat

1/2 cup fresh lemon juice

1 teaspoon fresh grated lemon zest (optional)

1 teaspoon vanilla extract or lemon brandy (see page 12)

1 prepared 8-inch crumb crust (graham cracker, shortbread, or chocolate)

1 pint fresh blueberries, straw-berries, blackberries, or rasp-berries, cleaned

• Serves 6

Lemon Chocolate Truffles

1 cup plus 2 tablespoons heavy cream

3/4 cup (1 1/2 sticks) unsalted butter

2 1/4 pounds bittersweet or semi-sweet chocolate, chopped

3/4 cup sour cream

6 tablespoons Grand Marnier, Lemoncello, or rum

1/4 cup finely grated lemon zest

1 1/2 cups unsweetened cocoa powder

- Makes about 6 dozen

I cooked for many years before I gathered up my courage and made chocolates. I bit the bullet one Christmas and made them for presents, and guess what? It wasn't so hard. If you don't have time to roll these truffles in cocoa powder, simply put cocoa and nuts in the bottom of the pan before you pour in the melted chocolate, then sprinkle more nuts and cocoa on top before chilling. Cut into squares as you would fudge. They won't be as elegant, but the taste is still out of this world. Do yourself a favor and use only the best chocolate; you will think you are eating $25-a-pound chocolates.

෫ඛ

Bring cream and butter to a boil in a heavy saucepan. Lower heat and stir until butter melts. Add chocolate, stirring until chocolate is melted and mixture is smooth. Remove from heat.

Whisk in sour cream, liquor, and lemon zest. Pour into a greased 9 x 13-inch baking dish. Refrigerate for 2 hours.

Spread cocoa powder on a jelly roll pan lined with foil. Using a 1 1/2-tablespoon scoop, scoop out the truffle mixture, mounding slightly, and drop onto the pan. When you have used all the truffle mixture, roll each ball in the cocoa powder. Store these in covered container in refrigerator.

Pears Poached in Port

This is another recipe that makes a nice presentation on a dessert table. Let the pears sit overnight in the reduced poaching liquid and they will turn a pretty red color. Serve with a cookie or two and maybe a dollop of whipped cream. If you prefer, you can omit the port and poach the pears in a lemon, sugar and spice mixture and add a bit of red food color.

&a

Mix together all ingredients except pears in a stainless steel saucepan large enough to hold pears comfortably. Bring to a boil and simmer for 15 minutes.

Peel pears but leave whole, with stems. Drop them into port mixture. Keeping liquid at a simmer, cook, turning occasionally, until pears are tender. Cooking time will vary depending on type of pear and degree of ripeness.

With a slotted spoon remove pears to a glass bowl. Boil liquid until reduced to a syrupy consistency. Pour over pears and refrigerate overnight, turning once to insure uniform color. Serve at room temperature, with a bit of syrup spooned on top.

1$1/2$ cups port wine

$1/2$ cup granulated sugar

2 cups water

Zest from 1 lemon

Juice from 1 lemon

2 cinnamon sticks

1 tablespoon whole cloves

6 pears, ripe but still firm

- Serves 6

Index